Understanding CBT

To Basia, Henry, Susanah and Simon.
For Pimpus, Monty, Chang and Singalino
who are a source of continuous joy.

KASIA

To Kate, who has supported me for three decades.

STEPHEN

Understanding CBT

Develop your own toolkit to reduce stress and increase well-being

KASIA SZYMANSKA
and STEPHEN PALMER

KoganPage

LONDON PHILADELPHIA NEW DELHI

Publisher's note

Every possible effort has been made to ensure that the information contained in this book is accurate at the time of going to press, and the publishers and authors cannot accept responsibility for any errors or omissions, however caused. No responsibility for loss or damage occasioned to any person acting, or refraining from action, as a result of the material in this publication can be accepted by the editor, the publisher or either of the authors.

First published in Great Britain and the United States in 2012 by Kogan Page Limited

120 Pentonville Road	1518 Walnut Street, Suite 1100	4737/23 Ansari Road
London N1 9JN	Philadelphia PA 19102	Daryaganj
United Kingdom	USA	New Delhi 110002
www.koganpage.com		India

© Kasia Szymanska and Stephen Palmer, 2012

The right of Kasia Szymanska and Stephen Palmer to be identified as the authors of this work has been asserted by them in accordance with the Copyright, Designs and Patents Act 1988.

ISBN   978 0 7494 5966 6
E-ISBN   978 0 7494 5967 3

British Library Cataloguing-in-Publication Data

A CIP record for this book is available from the British Library.

Library of Congress Cataloging-in-Publication Data

Palmer, Stephen.
    Understanding CBT : develop your own toolkit to reduce stress and increase well-being / Stephen Palmer, Kasia Szymanska.
        p. cm.
    Includes bibliographical references.
    ISBN 978-0-7494-5966-6 – ISBN 978-0-7494-5967-3 (ebook)   1. Job stress.
2. Cognitive therapy.   3. Stress management.   I. Szymanska, Kasia.   II. Title.
    HF5548.85.P35 2012
    158.7'2–dc23
                                                                            2011052736

Typeset by Graphicraft Ltd, Hong Kong
Printed and bound in India by Replika Press Pvt Ltd

Contents

Introduction

Is this book for you?

Do you recognize any of the items below in yourself?

- Stress and anxiety.
- Panic.
- Anxiety related problems such as agoraphobia, social phobia or dental phobia.
- Worry.
- Traumatic stress triggered by a frightening event.
- Depression and low mood.
- Physical pain such as backache which you find hard to live with.
- Insomnia or early awakening.
- Anger and irritability.
- As a parent you feel guilty about your behaviour towards your children.
- Eating disorders or just comfort eating under stress.
- Obsessive compulsive disorder such as constant checking or secret rituals in order to prevent an illness or disaster taking place.
- Rigid perfectionism which drives you and your colleagues crazy.
- Habit problems, such as smoking and biting your nails.
- Substance misuse including drinking too much alcohol to help you cope.

- Procrastination with important tasks.
- Low self-esteem.
- Unable to cope with criticism.
- Poor time management.
- Passive aggressive behaviour instead of being assertive with your colleagues or manager.

Let's be realistic, we are all fallible and it is likely that you may recognize one or two items above in yourself or perhaps a member of your family whom you are currently concerned about. Otherwise why did you pick this book up? (Of course, you may have been attracted by the excellent book cover.) Or perhaps you have heard about cognitive behavioural therapy and coaching and you are curious to find out more about this topic. Whatever the reason, hopefully this book will provide some of the answers.

The good news is that the cognitive behavioural approach to therapy (or in the case of this book, coaching, if it is a work-related performance issue), can help a person to tackle the items previously listed. It really is suitable for tackling anxiety-related problems and depression.

It is a psycho-educational approach. In other words, the qualified practitioner explains to the client the psychological theory under-pinning the techniques that can be used to deal with the problems. This transparency and matter of fact approach is one of the hall-marks of cognitive behavioural therapy and coaching. This book will provide you with information about a range of problems, many of which you can tackle yourself if you use the toolkit of techniques described in this book.

Origins of cognitive behavioural therapy

Modern day cognitive behavioural therapy is based on the principles of cognitive therapy which were developed back in the 1960s by an American psychiatrist, Dr Aaron T Beck. In the UK therapists took techniques from behaviour therapy and integrated and adapted them with cognitive therapy. Behaviour therapy helped a client to get used to anxiety triggering situations such as being phobic about travelling on trains by exposing the client to the situation. In this case they would get back on the train. After a short while the client found that their anxiety subsided. In the UK, gradually the approach became known as cognitive behaviour therapy (CBT). In the past 50 years it has gone from strength to strength both in the UK and worldwide. Its benefits are widely referred to in the media and it is the treatment of choice in the NHS because it has a proven track record of being effective, a record that is based on scientific research. This approach is constantly being updated; the focus of this research is on what works and for whom. The approach has also been adapted to the field of coaching to enhance performance, increase resilience, reduce stress and improve well-being.

It's really about learning the right skills

If you are learning to drive a car, your instructor will teach you the driving skills and techniques to help you to be a safe and competent driver. To be competent in using a computer you need to develop the correct computing skills. Equally to deal with psychological problems you need to learn the right skills to help yourself.

Our goal in writing this book is to use our combined expertise as qualified cognitive behavioural psychotherapists and registered psychologists to teach you these strategies, techniques and skills that can be applied to the issues that you are troubled about. As with the acquisition of any new sets of skills, it does take time to become familiar with any new methods. However, with perseverance and effort your proficiency and confidence in applying these skills will get you the results that you want. Essentially this book gives you a tool kit overflowing with the skills needed to initiate and maintain changes in your life; these are tools for life.

What are the principles behind this system?

There are two main principles that underpin this cognitive behavioural approach. The first is based on thinking skills and draws on the works of the Stoic philosophers, in particular Epictetus who suggested that people, 'are not disturbed by things, but by the view they take of them'. Much later Shakespeare wrote, 'Why, then 'tis none to you; for there is nothing either good or bad but thinking makes it so.' More recently Mahatma Gandhi said that 'A man is but the product of his thoughts, what he thinks, he becomes.' In other words, we make ourselves content or distressed depending upon how we view ourselves interacting with the world around us.

While the second principle regards our actions – or what we do or don't do – this is largely influenced by our thinking processes. For example, if you make the choice to exercise on a dreary winter morning it's because you believe or think it will do you good and be of some benefit to you, not because you are thinking 'I loathe exercise and would rather have an extra hour in bed!'

How to get the most out of this book

This book was written so you can dip in at any point to understand a particular topic of interest. However, we suggest that reading Chapters 1 and 2 would be a good start in understanding what the cognitive behavioural approach is all about, otherwise it may be a little unclear why we are spending so much time looking at your thinking.

The CBT approach provides a toolkit of techniques that are applied within a framework which we cover later in this book. The techniques will help you to dejunk your head of unhelpful, stress and anxiety inducing, performance interfering, resilience reducing thoughts and beliefs and develop helpful, stress and anxiety busting, performance enhancing and resilience increasing beliefs.

We suggest that the next Activity is worth undertaking as it may encourage you to stay focused on your goals.

Listing Your Goals for Reading This Book

Consider why you want to read this book and what you are hoping to achieve. Perhaps you want to overcome a phobia, manage panic attacks, stop procrastinating, give presentations at work, become more relaxed.
List below your goals and objectives:

- Goal 1:

- Goal 2:

- Goal 3:

- Goal 4:

- Goal 5:

- Goal 6:

- Goal 7:

- Goal 8:

Before you start reading a chapter, return to this goal list to remind yourself what you are hoping to achieve in reading this book. When you finish reading the chapter, return again to this goal list and reflect upon your progress. Revise this goal list if necessary.

Caveat

There is an important caveat to this self-help book. If you are suffering from anxiety or depression or other distressing psychological or physical symptoms, don't suffer in silence. Do seriously consider consulting your medical practitioner or qualified psychologist or psychotherapist. If you attempt a technique from this book and find it anxiety-provoking or overwhelming, then stop using it.

Chapter One
How does the cognitive behaviour approach work?

The key ideas behind this approach are as follows.

The link between thoughts and feelings

The cognitive behaviour approach works on the principle that our perceptions and thoughts greatly influence how we react to situations, both in terms of what we do and how we feel. We all have hundreds of automatic thoughts that go through our minds every day and we don't necessarily pay attention to most of them. If we did, we could spend too much time thinking about thinking, which is a sure-fire strategy to make us feel uncomfortable and far too introspective.

Nevertheless, there is one set of thoughts that we should pay attention to. These are negative or unhelpful automatic thoughts, the kind of thoughts that over time can lead to stress, procrastination, worry and more challenging psychological problems, such as depression and anxiety. Sometimes we call them NATs, which is short for negative automatic thoughts.

Let's take an example. If you worry about speaking out in a meeting because you are anxious that you will say something stupid and make a fool of yourself, you are more than likely to feel stressed. The key link here is between your thoughts (NATs) and feelings. Equally a person who has just lost their job after having been made redundant may think, 'I'll never find another job, my career is over.' This kind of thinking can make them feel depressed.

The link between thoughts, feeling, behaviours and physical responses

Negative thinking can also impact on how we act in a situation and upon our physical (physiological) responses. So going back to the first example, if you feel stressed and are having negative thoughts in a meeting, this can have consequences; it impacts on your overall performance in the meeting and may lead to possible palpitations or sweaty palms (physical reactions). In the second example, feeling depressed can lead to inactivity. If you believe strongly that you are not going to find another job, you are not likely to look for another one (behaviour). This may even affect your ability to sleep well (behaviour), and this can then impact on your body so you may start to feel aches or tension (physical response).

One way of understanding this connection between these four areas is to use the diagram shown below. Going back to the first example, the link between negative thoughts, feelings, behaviour and physical responses is outlined below.

Each key area or modality impacts upon the other. In this case negative thoughts can increase one's emotional feelings of anxiety; the anxiety in turn increases your physical responses of tension and sweaty palms. These responses are likely to impact upon your (behavioural) performance.

FIGURE 1.1

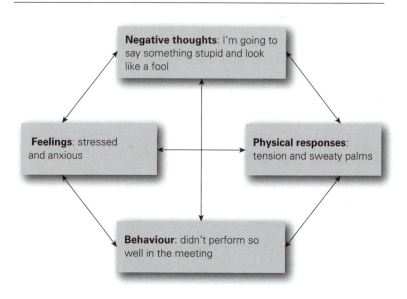

The link between current and childhood experiences

Sometimes what happened in our childhood and adolescence can still influence how we deal with our current experiences. The negative thoughts we covered in the diagram above are 'surface thoughts' which are quite easy to access (literally hear in your mind) and change. However, just below the surface thoughts or NATs are what we call intermediate and core beliefs. These may be more difficult to access and often have developed during childhood and adolescence. For example, if you had a critical parent or teacher, you may have been told that you were stupid if you made a mistake. Let's see how this looks in terms of the three levels of beliefs:

NATs: I've made a mistake. That's not good. What will they think of me?

Intermediate belief: If I make a mistake, then I'm stupid.

Core belief: I'm stupid.

And the catch is that your parent or teacher may sadly have died but years later, as an adult, you are still walking around with these beliefs, ready to be triggered by events.

Usually the intermediate beliefs come in the form of an 'if... then' or 'unless... then' structure. They can also consist of rules such as, 'I must always perform well.' It's easy to see how intermediate beliefs can help to determine how we lead our lives.

Core beliefs are often a part of the intermediate belief. In the example above: 'If I make a mistake, then I'm stupid.' the 'I'm stupid' is the core belief. These beliefs are usually quite rigid. Other common examples are 'I'm useless' or 'I'm bad'. We all have core beliefs, often a mixture of positive (eg I'm intelligent) and negative (eg I'm stupid) ideas. They can lie dormant and then can be triggered as a result of life experiences. A stressful event at work may trigger negative core beliefs such as 'People can't be trusted', whereas occasionally a good experience could trigger a positive core belief such as 'People are trustworthy'.

The diagram below illustrates how we can link our understanding of our current issues with our childhood. In this example, Ellie was bullied by her team leader; he undermined her work and told her that her performance was not up to scratch. To Ellie this reminded her of the time she was bullied in secondary school, as she remembered a teacher who constantly criticised the quality of her schoolwork. At school she worked hard to ensure that she did not make any mistakes, but despite this the teacher compared her work negatively to that handed in by other pupils and always wrote at least one negative comment on her homework assignments. Ellie developed the notion that she was inadequate. As an adult she performed well in her job, until she was moved to a different department and met with her current team leader. His criticism of her work triggered her underlying core belief: 'I'm inadequate.' Even though she worked extra hard to prove to herself that she could do well, she begun to feel as helpless as she did when she was back at school.

FIGURE 1.2

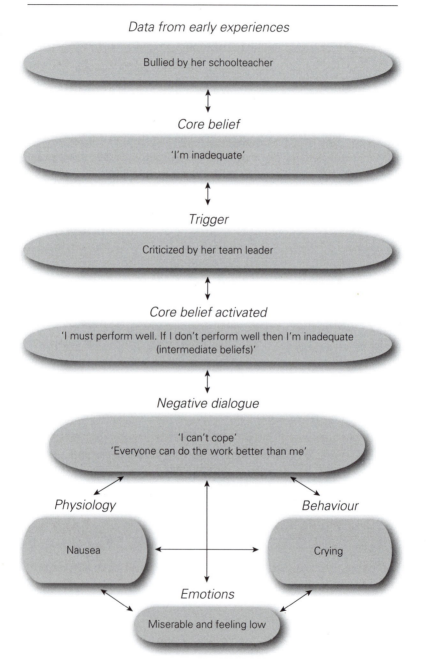

Data from early experiences

Bullied by her schoolteacher

Core belief

'I'm inadequate'

Trigger

Criticized by her team leader

Core belief activated

'I must perform well. If I don't perform well then I'm inadequate (intermediate beliefs)'

Negative dialogue

'I can't cope'
'Everyone can do the work better than me'

Physiology

Nausea

Behaviour

Crying

Emotions

Miserable and feeling low

This diagram is like a map that helps us to piece together why Ellie is reacting in the way she is now to the current situation she finds herself in. If she was in therapy this diagram would be known as a case conceptualization. Mapping our experience, beliefs, behaviour, emotions and physical reactions really helps to provide us with an insight into the problems we are distressed about and is the gateway to choosing a new thinking and behavioural approach to dealing with issues.

In the following chapters we discuss how you can learn to deal with your problems using this approach. In Chapter 2 we start by providing more examples of the link between thoughts, feelings, behaviours and physiology before looking at how you can work with negative automatic thoughts (NATs), intermediate beliefs and core beliefs.

Chapter Two
How to recognize and manage unhelpful or inflexible thinking patterns

Being able to identify, understand and then deconstruct your own negative thought processes and their influence on your moods/emotions and actions is a critical part of cognitive behavioural self-help and self-coaching.

In this chapter we focus on the strategies to identify and challenge negative or inflexible thoughts before moving onto recognizing and challenging intermediate and core beliefs, with the aim of supporting you in the goal of becoming your own cognitive behavioural therapist/coach. We also provide a simple cognitive behavioural model to introduce you to the approach.

What are negative automatic thoughts?

Negative automatic thoughts (NATs) are often referred to as 'pop-up' thoughts and they can seem believable and reasonable although often difficult to articulate as they are slippery and hard to pin down. In order to become your own self-therapist or coach it is important to train yourself to become aware of your NATs and thinking styles. This takes a little time and practice.

These NATs can include negative thoughts and images, such as 'I'm a stupid person' or 'Everyone hates me', or a combination of both (eg picturing yourself making a mess of a presentation and thinking, 'I really mustn't make mistakes when I give this presentation. I don't want to make a fool of myself, my manager will be there'). The key features of these thoughts and images are that they can pop into your mind quickly, which is why they are often referred to as automatic or pop-up thoughts. Sometimes they can be unwritten contracts that your colleagues have no knowledge about, such as 'Everyone should acknowledge what I've said.' In addition one thought can lead to another and then another at such a great speed that you can quickly make yourself feel stressed without much effort. Take the image of 'making a mess of a presentation'. This can be the trigger to a protracted negative downward spiral; for example this image can lead to worries about your job, then you picture being made redundant (because your presentation skills are so bad), etc.

Only one negative thought or picture in your head can lead to a stress-inducing spiral, from an initial concern about a presentation to an outcome that has nothing to do with the original thought or image.

The key point to remember here is to identify and work with the NATs that leads to negative mood states, such as stress, anger and anxiety, and the accompanying unhelpful behaviours, such as putting off completing tasks, drinking too much alcohol in order to cope, or avoidance of people or places.

Here we are only concerned with the negative thoughts that contribute to psychological distress – the thoughts that do not occur as a result of rational reasoning. So, it may be reasonable to assume that you are going to make a mess of giving a presentation if you have made a mess of all the other presentations you have given. However, if you have never given a presentation, it is reasonable to spend a certain amount of time preparing for the presentation and to feel a bit nervous and think, 'I'm really going to do the best that I can do, I'm prepared for this', but it is not helpful to imagine yourself failing or worrying that you will blush, shake or be judged negatively by your audience. This negative thinking only serves to make you feel more nervous (the connection between thinking and feeling) and can impair your performance, ultimately leading to a self-fulfilling prophecy (ie 'I knew I would make a mess and I did').

The bottom line here is this: thinking in this way is performance blocking and it does not help to achieve your goal.

Identifying such thoughts

As we mentioned in Chapter 1, knowing and articulating what you are thinking about at any time is not easy to do. To be able to identify your negative automatic thoughts takes time to do and is a learning process; after all you don't expect to learn to type at once or drive a car immediately, so why should you know how to identify and challenge your negative thoughts?

Heightening awareness of negative thinking

To become more aware of your negative thinking, consider the following.

Keep a brief and regular diary of the experiences that you recognize as contributing to negative thinking and negative emotions. Try and write about the experience as soon as it has happened.

Below is an excerpt from Sarah's diary; she was stressed at work and worried about the next round of redundancies:

> 'Went to get a cappuccino from the coffee machine on the 4th floor, met Stuart the HR manager at the machine, he seemed really preoccupied and distant. Am worried, why was he like that? He didn't even look at me, he knows something about me, it's the redundancies. He knows that I will be made redundant, that is why he is behaving strangely with me. Feel sick, tight chest, butterflies in my stomach, must update my CV.'

Aim to differentiate between negative thoughts and feelings. In this example, the negative thoughts are, 'Why was he distant? Does he know something about me? Is it because of the redundancies? Maybe he knows that I'm going to be made redundant and that was why he behaved strangely with me. I must update my CV.'

The consequences for Sarah of thinking in this way are feeling anxious as well as the physical sensations of sickness, butterflies and tightness in the chest. This is known as the B-C (Belief-Consequences) connection, and the underlying premise here is that the way you perceive a situation or think about it leads to how you feel about it, accompanying physical sensations and what you do about it. In addition we can add an 'A' to this sequence, where the 'A' stands for the activating or initial event that triggered the thinking process, emotional/physical reaction(s) and action(s).

Table 2.1 illustrates an A-B-C sequence. Recognizing emotions is often easier to do then recognizing negative thoughts: in the main we can all recognize that we feel angry or sad, without always knowing initially why we feel this way.

If you do not have the time to write about the experience as soon as possible, then when you do have time and pen and paper to hand, close your eyes and remember as vividly as possible the situation that caused you distress. Then jot down the key negative thoughts and emotions associated with it.

FIGURE 2.1   The A-B-C connection

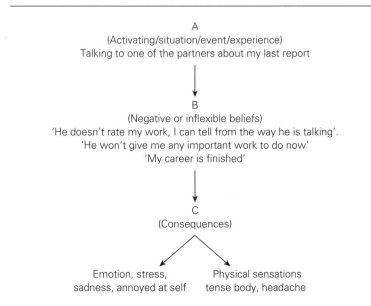

A
(Activating/situation/event/experience)
Talking to one of the partners about my last report

B
(Negative or inflexible beliefs)
'He doesn't rate my work, I can tell from the way he is talking'.
'He won't give me any important work to do now'
'My career is finished'

C
(Consequences)

Emotion, stress, sadness, annoyed at self

Physical sensations tense body, headache

TABLE 2.1 Some A-B-C connections

A: event	B: negative thoughts about the event	C: reactions to your thoughts
Conversation with partner about our relationship	He looks bored He hates me	Feeling depressed, sinking feeling in my stomach
Talking to my boss about difficult team member	He doesn't understand what I am talking about He is probably going to side with her He thinks I'm the trouble maker	Feeling anxious, want to get away
Looking at my untidy desk	I can't do this I should keep it tidy all the time What's wrong with me?	Feeling overwhelmed, put off tidying desk and get on with doing the report
Interview for new job	I'm going to make a hash of the interview They probably have much better candidates then me	Feeling stressed, butterflies in my stomach Need to run to the toilet
Participating in a conference call	My voice will shake I'll dry up They'll think I'm not up to the job	Anxious so try to get out of conference call
At home due to illness	I'll never catch up at work now My team are having to do my job, that's terrible	Feeling guilty, worrying more about workload
Working long hours	I'll never finish this work Everyone seems to be more efficient than me I can't do this job	Feeling stressed, and apprehensive about tomorrow

To improve your skills in identifying negative thinking use the examples listed in the box below and aim to highlight the negative thoughts, feelings and if applicable the physical sensations associated with the experience or event. The aim is to make the A-B-C connection and then to apply the strategies outlined in this chapter to work on your negative automatic beliefs.

Identify the link between negative thoughts and feelings

Example 1

Joe has been off sick from work for six weeks but is due to return to work in the next week. As soon as he thinks about his first day back, he starts to feel sick, his stomach churns and he imagines his colleagues asking him where has been and why he was off from work for so long. He finds it hard to think of an answer that will be acceptable to his colleagues and worries how his manager will react to the reduced hours he will be working.

Example 2

Dawn finds her job as an administrator very stressful. She has two people working for her, one of whom is not pulling their weight. She wants to confront him but is worried that he will ignore her or respond aggressively. She pictures herself confronting him and believes that she will mix up her words, blush and therefore look stupid. She is worried that other people in the open-plan office may overhear her conversation and see her blushing and think she is not up to the job.

Example 3

Paula needs to tell her manager that her workload is too high. She is overloaded with work, while some of the other personal assistants in the office seem to have time to spare. Everyone knows that her manager can be difficult and has little time to spare for one-to-one meetings with staff. She imagines that the meeting will be a disaster and lies awake for hours before falling asleep thinking about the meeting. Now she finds it hard to fall asleep before midnight. On the day of their meeting, she feels tired from lack of sleep, her heart is racing and she has a picture of her manager being brusque with her and her starting to cry, which means that she has messed up the meeting and is now truly making a fool of herself.

Thinking errors

Once you have become more proficient at recognizing your own negative thoughts, it can be helpful to view your negative thoughts in terms of 'thinking errors'. These are categories of common thinking patterns that cognitive and behavioural practitioners have identified as contributing to negative emotions. They are listed in Figure 2.2. We have often found that for many of our clients, just knowing that such a list of thinking errors exists helps them to normalize their thinking and accept that they are not the only ones who have negative thoughts and difficulties in managing certain life experiences.

Developing the skills to manage and challenge your negative thinking

Having identified your negative thoughts the next step is to assess their legitimacy. Hypothesis one is that they are legitimate and accurate and that you should feel the way you feel, and hypothesis two is that they are inaccurate and impacting negatively on your mood. One of the most productive ways to do this is to use a 'thought form'. This provides a structure for processing your negative thoughts. An example of a completed thought form using the example above of Sarah is provided in Table 2.2. A blank automatic thought form is provided in Appendix A. In completing the form the first step is to make and write down the A-B-C connection. Practise this first before going on to identify the thinking errors related to your negative beliefs. Then go on to dispute and challenge your negative thoughts using the Socratic questions in the next section then develop more realistic, flexible, helpful thoughts relating to the issue concerned. Finally develop new ways of dealing with the situation.

FIGURE 2.2   Common thinking errors

All-or-nothing thinking: appraising experiences on the basis of extremes.

'He is always angry' or 'I'm always last in line for promotion.'

Labelling: using negative labels to describe yourself and others.

'I'm so stupid' or 'I'm a failure.'

Mind reading: believing that you know what others are thinking about you.

'He knows that I haven't finished that assignment' or 'She is ignoring me because she is angry with me.'

Fortune telling: believing that you know what the future holds.

'My job won't be there when I go back' or 'I'll never find another job.'

Emotional reasoning: being unable to differentiate feelings from facts.

'I feel anxious, therefore this meeting will be a disaster' or 'I feel guilty therefore it must be my fault.'

Personalization: taking things personally.

'I don't get the bonus because I'm not good enough' or 'We didn't get the contract because my presentation was rubbish.'

Demands: being demanding of yourself and others, using words such as, 'should', 'must', 'ought to'.

'I *must* perform perfectly' or 'I *should* be able to manage my staff.'

Low frustration tolerance or 'I can't stand it-itis': finding it difficult to tolerate difficult situations.

'I can't stand this' or 'I can't bear this.'

Magnification: blowing situations out of proportion.

'If I don't secure this contract, I might as well give in my notice.'

Phoneyism: thinking that you will get found out.

'If I don't do this task well, he'll know I'm a fraud, or 'If I succumb to the pressure, everyone will know I'm not cut out for this job.'

What if?: asking yourself 'what if?' without developing a helpful answer.

'What if I can't cope?' or 'What if I'll never stop worrying?'

TABLE 2.2   Sarah's automatic thought form

Situation A	Your negative thoughts about the situation B	Your feelings and physical responses C	Develop realistic thoughts D	Effective new way of dealing with the situation E
Meeting Stuart at the coffee machine.	Why is Stuart so distant? He knows I will be made redundant. I have to update my CV as I'll be out of a job soon.	Feel sick. Feel anxious. Tight chest.	I'm not a mind reader: there are tons of other reasons he may be behaving this way. If I think in this way I won't feel anxious or need to update my CV, which frankly is just a waste of my precious time. Stop jumping to conclusions. *The questions Sarah asked herself which linked to her thinking errors:* *Am I mind reading here?* *Jumping to conclusions?* *How do I know for a fact that my interpretation of the situation is correct?* *Could there be other explanations? What could they be? Have I been wrong before?*	Stop thinking in this way, I have no proof, concentrate on the task in hand.

The process of challenging and working through your negative thoughts

Using Socratic questioning to tease out your negative thoughts works. Based on the Socratic method developed by the 5th-century BC philosopher Socrates, Socratic questions enable you to develop different perspectives, or put more simply to think outside the box. The following list of Socratic questions can be applied to the process of challenging/restructuring negative thoughts:

- Where is the evidence to support my negative thinking?
- What are the advantages and disadvantages of my negative thoughts?
- Would my negative thoughts, if presented before a judge, stand up in a court of law?
- Where does my negative thinking get me?
- Would I encourage a friend or a colleague to think in the same way? If no, why not?
- Is my thinking logical?
- Am I taking matters too personally?
- Am I confusing probabilities with possibilities?
- Am I confusing feelings with facts?
- Am I jumping to the worst possible outcome?
- Am I being too demanding of myself or others?
- Am I aiming for perfectionism?
- Am I overemphasizing my control of the situation?
- Am I making the situation appear more awful than it really is?
- Am I mind reading?
- Am I applying double standards?
- Is my thinking too extreme?
- What is the middle ground here?
- Am I telling myself that I can't stand something, which in reality I am standing?

Sarah links her negative thoughts to the common thinking errors as described in Figure 2.2 before using a selection of Socratic questions to tackle her negative automatic thoughts. She asks herself if she knows for certain that her interpretation of the situation is true? Could there be another explanation for his behaviour? For example, was Stuart distracted because he was tired, was he day dreaming? In addition she asks herself if she had jumped to conclusions before and if she was always correct in her previous assumptions about situations. Sarah could also ask herself, 'Where is my negative thinking getting me?'

In the final stage of completing the automatic thought form, Sarah outlined a new way of managing her situation under E, a proactive stance which is not underpinned by negative thinking, rather realistic thinking and behaving.

When using automatic thought forms it is important that you work through the issue systematically and in writing without missing out any of the sections. Always try to use one automatic form per issue.

Intermediate beliefs

It is very likely that Kim (who we meet next) also held some beliefs in between her negative dialogue and core beliefs. For example, 'If my pay rise is denied, then this proves I'm not OK,' or 'Unless I'm good at my job, then I'm not OK.' 'If-then' and 'unless-then' beliefs are known as underlying assumptions and are considered to be intermediate beliefs. They can be negative or positive and generally include the core belief. Intermediate beliefs may also include demanding rules of life the person rigidly holds on to, such as 'I must perform well.' Intermediate beliefs can also include unvocalized/unwritten contracts such as 'Others must treat me well' or 'If I do someone a favour then they should reciprocate.'

Through discussion we encourage our clients to develop new intermediate beliefs, which are noted down. For example:

- 'If my pay rise is denied, then it may signify nothing about me.'

- 'I strongly prefer to perform well but realistically I don't have to.'

- 'I am treated well by others most of the time.'

- 'If I do someone a favour then it's preferable they reciprocate, but they don't have to.'

Often intermediate beliefs determine how you lead your life, as the rules, unwritten contracts and underlying assumptions influence your behaviour with friends, family, colleagues and strangers and with organisations you deal with too. It's worth looking out for them the next time you become stressed and note them down.

Working with core beliefs

In the previous chapter we introduced core beliefs. Here we focus on the strategies you can use to challenge your core beliefs. To recap: if, for example, your parents instilled in you the belief that you have to always do tasks perfectly and you were praised as a child only for achieving good academic results, you may have a perfection core belief. In the main this thinking style may aid you in your professional and personal life. However, if due to economic circumstances, you are made redundant from a job you value, it is likely that you will feel low and distressed because it's very important for you to do well. In this case it's important to tackle the core beliefs or roots of the issue and the negative automatic thoughts associated with the issue(s) involved. It is not always necessary to work with your core beliefs, unless having read this chapter you recognize that your past experiences have had an impact on how you think and behave now. Otherwise working with NATs and intermediate beliefs is more than sufficient.

The diagram that follows shows how Kim who was treated very differently to her three brothers as a child developed an 'I'm not OK' core belief. Her parents favoured her brothers and Kim believed that she was 'invisible' to her parents. As an adult Kim worked in HR and some of her male colleagues were paid more than her, so Kim asked for a pay rise, which her manager denied; his reasoning for this was lame. To Kim this denial activated her 'I'm not OK' core belief and lead her to lose confidence in her ability.

FIGURE 2.3   Link between early experiences, core beliefs and automatic thoughts

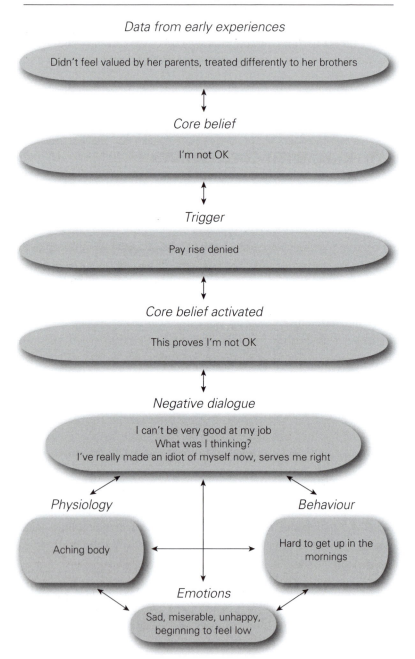

Core belief or a form of self-prejudice?

Dr Christine Padesky (1990) uses the metaphor of self-prejudice to describe core beliefs and their impact on your cognitive processes and actions. To understand this link, below is an excerpt from a coaching session focusing on self-prejudice.

Coach: Before we go on to address and modify your 'not good enough core belief', I wonder if we could talk for 20 minutes or so about prejudice. Can you tell me, do you know a family member, friend or colleague who has a strong prejudice which you personally don't agree with?

Coachee: Yes my brother-in-law David. He is always telling us that all women are terrible drivers.

Coach: OK, if you can put yourself in David's shoes, I wonder what David would say if he was driving and saw an accident involving a woman driver?

Coachee: He would say that it was her fault.

Coach: OK and how would he respond to statistics highlighting the increase in accidents over the past year?

Coachee: He would probably say that it's down to more women drivers being on the road.

Coach: And finally how would he respond to a woman driver on the motorway who stays in the overtaking lane?

Coachee: She has no idea about the Highway Code and she is stupid.

Coach: It does seem that David has some pretty strongly held beliefs about women drivers; from my perspective he seems to have a tendency to jump to conclusions, misinterpretation and labelling women drivers without being in possession of all the facts.

Coachee: Yes I can see that, I feel sorry for my sister sometimes!

Coach: Mmm, if you were to support your sister here and help David to see women drivers in a more realistic light, I wonder how you would proceed.

Coachee: Well I would most probably sit down with him over a coffee or even in the pub and then get him to prove to me that he is right. Then I would use my sister's driving history to substantiate my views. She has never had an accident, unlike David who was caught speeding two years ago.

Coach: Sounds like an excellent idea; can you see a link between what we are talking about here and your own core belief?

Coachee: Hmm, the idea that my core belief, 'I'm not good enough' is possibly a kind of prejudice'?

Coach: Yes a prejudice that you have reinforced over the past ten years with your negative thinking. For example, when you were one of 50 people made redundant instead of looking at the obvious reasons why the redundancy happened you immediately decided it was because you weren't doing a good enough job.

The coach and the coachee then go onto view the core belief as a prejudice which the coachee needs to challenge.

One of the advantages of thinking of a core belief as a prejudice is that we all recognize prejudices and how they can exert a powerful and intrinsic influence on our lives, so treating a core belief as prejudice which needs to be disputed and then replaced with a preferential viewpoint is a starting point for the change process.

Identifying your own core belief

The tool commonly used to identify your own core belief(s) is known as the downward arrow technique, an example of its application is highlighted below:

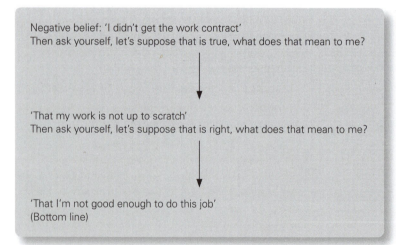

Negative belief: 'I didn't get the work contract'
Then ask yourself, let's suppose that is true, what does that mean to me?

'That my work is not up to scratch'
Then ask yourself, let's suppose that is right, what does that mean to me?

'That I'm not good enough to do this job'
(Bottom line)

Here the bottom line or the core belief is that the individual believes that 'I'm not good enough.'

Below is another example taken from a session with a coachee who demanded perfection in all aspects of her life, which ultimately led to an increase in stress in her role as an HR manager.

Coachee: This report needs to be perfect.

Coach: Let's suppose that it doesn't meet the mark and your boss finds some minor typos in the report, what does that mean to you?

Coachee: He'll think I'm not up to scratch.

Coach: OK and if he does really think that, what will that mean to you?

Coachee: I'm a rubbish person.

In this case the coachee's core belief is 'I'm rubbish.'

The aim is now to modify core beliefs. If you have more than one core belief use the strategies outlined below to work with all of them, but focus on modifying one core belief at a time.

Modifying core beliefs

There are a number of complementary strategies which you can use to weaken core beliefs. Here we start by looking at the pros and cons of holding onto the belief, 'I'm not good enough.'

Strategy 1

Focus on the costs and benefits of holding onto your core belief. (Always complete the exercises outlined in this chapter in writing.)

Strategy 2

Complete an historical test of your core belief. To do this, divide your life into manageable sections and then look at the historical evidence which supports your belief and then evidence which does not support your belief. For guidance see the example overleaf:

TABLE 2.3

Evidence which supports the notion that I'm not good enough	Evidence which goes against this idea
Age 0–10 Could not speak English when started primary school	I developed normally as a baby and child I learnt English as a second language within a couple of months of starting school
Age 11–18 Failed A level in RE	I passed 2 A levels and got into uni
Age 19–29 Made redundant once	I have a nice flat and a mortgage and survived the recent round of redundancies

Overall summary of positive evidence:

Even though I didn't speak English until the age of five, I have achieved a lot; I actually did OK academically, I have my own flat and an OK job. This really points to the fact that I'm actually 'good enough'.

Doing a historical test of your core belief can be empowering. To reinforce your preferential viewpoint, jot down your summary on a piece of paper, carry it with you and read it regularly.

Strategy 3

The final strategy is a simple step-by-step process to change core beliefs.

- Step 1: Involves listing experiences which indicate that the core belief is not 100 per cent true.

- Step 2: Involves writing down a revised core belief based on your work from step 1 and/or information derived from strategies 1 and 2 and then listing new experiences that support the new revised core belief, if possible on a daily basis.

- Step 3: Involves rating your confidence in the revised belief on a regular basis.

Continuing on with the example of 'I'm not good enough', the process of working through the three steps is as follows:

Experiences which do not support my core belief (past and current):

- I got some good school reports.
- I passed about 90 per cent of my exams.
- I got into university.
- I have managed to stay in employment for most of my working life.
- My manager said that the report I wrote last week was insightful.

Based on step 1, I recognize that I am good enough, even though I don't always believe it; otherwise I would never have been able to list the experiences above. I'd like of think of myself as OK.
New core belief: I'm OK.

New recent experiences that support this. Aim to record positive experiences on a daily basis until you find that your confidence rating is at least over 50 per cent.

- One of my clients complimented me on the content of the report I wrote.
- My chat with the manager went well.
- I was able to explain my role to the person in HR.
- My colleague said that my telephone manner is good.

Confidence rating in 'I'm OK' based on a rating scale of 0 per cent (no confidence) to 100 per cent (total confidence).

Date and rating

_____

Date and rating

_____

(Adapted from Greenberger and Padesky, 1995)

Looking at the above example, the steps may seem to be quite simple. However, it is important to remember that transforming core beliefs can be a lengthy process. Use the strategies outlined on a regular basis until you notice that the potency of the old core belief(s) is eroded and your confidence in your new core belief(s) is increasing.

In the next chapter we focus on behavioural strategies which when used in combination with cognitive skills can greatly improve your chances of dealing with issues effectively.

Chapter Three
Behavioural techniques

It is very useful to identify and then modify negative thinking styles. However, that is just one aspect of the cognitive behavioural approach. Intellectual insight needs to be reinforced and the best way to do this is by giving it a go and actually doing something such as facing your fear. This 'doing' or behavioural component of cognitive behavioural therapy really helps the change process.

Take Patricia, who following her divorce was feeling miserable and sorry for herself. She had stopped meeting her friends and neglected her keep-fit classes, instead staying at home watching television, going over the divorce in her head and drinking a little too much wine. Over a period of weeks, Patricia began to recognize that she was stuck in a vicious cycle. The more time she spent at home doing very little apart from ruminating on the past, the more miserable she felt and her previous drive to keep herself busy was diminished to the extent that she was able to talk herself out of doing more very quickly. Recognizing this cycle was the first step towards change for Patricia, but it did not stop her from feeling miserable. Making the commitment to change her behaviour, doing more in the evenings and at weekends, helped her to feel happier, which in turn enabled her to reduce her alcohol consumption.

In this chapter we outline the kind of behavioural changes you can make and discuss the strategies that can be executed to change your behaviour, bearing in mind that any behavioural change requires motivation, a robust rationale or a good reason to change, skills, effort and finally regular practice to cement the new behaviour.

When considering a behaviour assignment, remember the acronym RESP:

- **R**obust rationale for the change is needed: what are your reasons for undertaking this change?
- **E**ffort: do you have the motivation and the determination to do this?
- **S**kills: do you have the necessary skills and resources to implement change?
- **P**ractice: any new behaviour requires practice in order for it to be integrated fully into everyday life.

If you recognize that change needs to happen but still remain ambivalent about it, consider using motivation imagery developed by Palmer and Neenan (1998) to improve your chances of implementation. First imagine your future in as much detail as possible without addressing this change. Consider how you will be feeling and what you will be doing. Then imagine how the future unfolds having made this change. After having worked hard to achieve it, consider how you feel and what you will be doing differently.

In this chapter we will be covering three main forms of behavioural change: active assignments and observational assignments, and the graded behavioural change that occurs under the first two.

Active assignments

These involve us actively testing out new realistic ways of thinking and behaving. By testing them out we can see if they are valid or not. We are unlikely to believe our new ideas unless we can monitor them and see if they are truly realistic from our perspective.

Example 1

Issue addressed

When stressed, Belinda began to triple-check all her work: she checked her written reports for any grammatical and spelling errors, and checked her e-mails for spelling mistakes and that she was sending then to the right people, and overall she believed that by doing so she was reducing the chances of making any errors. The impact of this excessive checking led to a magnification of her stress, increased her working hours, physical tension and demanding thinking such as 'I must get this right.'

Automatic negative thought targeted

If I don't triple-check my work it won't be right and it has to be.

Realistic response

If I check just once like most of my colleagues and as I did before, I'll have more time to complete my other work and hopefully won't need to stay late.

Behavioural assignment

Target two minor tasks a day, only check these once for the next 10 days before my coaching session.

Outcome

At the next coaching session, Belinda described feeling quite anxious initially when she only checked the work once: however after three days she found that her anxiety had subsided and that she was no longer concerned about any possible mistakes made. During the next session Belinda and the coach agreed to target three more significant tasks she would only check once.

Example 2

Issue addressed

Greg played guitar in his spare time and was due to play his first gig in the pub near his office. He had asked his work colleagues to come and see the band play. As the time for the gig drew close he began to feel quite nervous and worried that when under the spotlight he would forget his words, be unable to play and look ridiculous.

Automatic negative thought targeted

If I mess up I'll look really stupid and they'll all think I'm an amateur. I will never live it down.

Realistic response

Worrying about messing it up will just make it worse; I've been playing for over 10 years.

Behavioural assignment

To play a solo outside my flat on the main road for 20 minutes on a busy Saturday morning and then again outside the local train station.

Outcome

Greg found that when he started to play he felt a bit nervous. However, this feeling went away very quickly even though some people did stop to watch him. He was surprised to find that nobody said anything bad and in fact four people said that he had a great voice. His confidence in his ability increased and he recognized that looking stupid was very unlikely to happen. If it did happen he would remind himself that the criticism was far outweighed by the positive feedback he had received. He might even learn something useful if it was constructive feedback.

Observational assignments

Observational experiments usually take the form of surveys, constructed and conducted by the individual.

Example 1

Ivan worked as a medical representative for a large pharmaceutical company but was concerned that he did not fit the image of a representative. He had a strong accent and a birthmark on his face; he was worried that his potential clients would prejudge him negatively on the basis of his accent when on the phone making arrangements for face-to-face meetings; and that when he met with his clients they would focus more on his birthmark then the products he was selling. In addition he often compared himself with the other representatives, whom he described as 'more normal looking', which had the consequence of raising his overall level of unease. Here, Ivan and his coach initially worked on the negative impact of comparison before targeting the automatic negative thoughts using the survey method. They agreed on the following action: that he would survey 10 friends and colleagues in the next two weeks and ask them whether a) they prejudge people on the phone on the basis of their accent and b) they prejudge people on the basis of their appearance in professional situations. He recorded all the responses and discussed these in the next session. Of the 10 people surveyed no one said they prejudged people on the basis of their accent and only one said that they have judged people on the basis of their appearance. This person had a disability and tended to judge himself; however, he also added that once he engaged in conversation he no longer worried about what others thought of him.

Example 2

Steve balanced a busy professional and family life. He worked as an HR director within an international investment bank and had a hectic home life with three young children under the age of 10. Over the past two years he was experiencing problems falling asleep. He found that it took him over two hours to fall asleep, which he found frustrating, and the lack of sleep was catching up with him, so he was increasingly tired during the working day. On careful questioning it emerged that Steve was using the time before falling asleep to mentally go over his day at work and to plan his activities for the next couple of weeks. He said that this was the only time he had to himself and that he valued the opportunity to think about his role in HR. His coach suggested that there was a possible link between his thinking and his difficulty falling asleep, but Steve was reluctant to give up this period of 'constructive thinking'. For him this was the only time he could carve out of his busy life to reflect on his working day and as he purposefully didn't focus on negative aspects of his work, rather concentrating on future projects, he didn't see why it should have such a strong impact on his sleep.

His coach suggested a number of steps to test out his belief, the first being the observational assignment. He agreed to talk to six friends about their sleep hygiene and ask then specifically if a) they found it easy to fall asleep and b) if not, what they did to aid falling asleep. He was surprised to find that four of his friends had had or were experiencing sleep problems. Their remedies to this were to set aside the hour before bed to relax and prepare for bed without watching TV or reading and to keep a note pad by their bed to write down any ideas that popped into their head whilst trying to fall asleep.

When Steve said that he used the time in bed to think about work, all his friends agreed that he was wrong to do so. Step two involved Steve using the internet to find evidence to support his view that creative thinking was effective use of time in bed. When he reported back that the information he found did not support this idea, his final step was use the note pad strategy. He agreed to write down all his ideas on the note pad on his bedside table and instead of using his journey into work to answer his e-mails, to use this time to think about work projects. After some regular practice he found it easier to fall asleep more quickly.

The examples in this chapter have highlighted that by modifying our unhelpful thinking we may start to act behaviourally in a more desirable manner in order to achieve our goals.

Chapter Four
How to use imagery to cope with strong emotions and unhelpful thinking

Images or pictures, often in combination with negative perceptions and physical reactions, can perpetuate a number of different psychological issues outlined in this book from worry to anxiety and stress. Frequently images of events can lead to more powerful emotions than just thoughts about events, picturing a meeting you are chairing spiralling out of control, seeing yourself stumble over your words, your hands starting to shake, then seeing others looking at you. Wondering what is wrong with you is more likely to make you feel anxious as opposed to simply thinking about the meeting. While for individuals who have experienced a trauma, seeing the accident in their mind's eye, without actually wanting to, is another example.

Here we provide descriptions of how imagery techniques, in combination with other techniques, can be used to cope with some psychological problems. In 1984 Professor Arnold Lazarus, an American psychologist, highlighted the benefits of imagery strategies stating that:

> Through the proper use of mental imagery, one can achieve an immediate sense of self confidence, develop more energy and stamina and tap one's own mind for numerous productive purposes.

Lazarus also outlined exercises which can be used to improve your ability to apply imagery strategies effectively. Two exercises are listed below:

The candle

1 Relax and close your eyes

2 Imagine a dimly lit candle at the end of a dark room

3 Imagine a small flame

4 Does it grow brighter and dimmer in your mind's eye?

5 Practise for five minutes getting the flame to be brighter then dimmer

An object

1 Find an object

2 Examine the object until you know it in detail

3 Close your eyes and imagine that you are still studying the object

4 Do this for a couple of minutes

5 Now open your eyes and look at the initial object

6 Does your image differ from the object at all?

7 Repeat this process, and then repeat it again with a different object

The imagery techniques

The ones we will consider here include compassion focused imagery, coping imagery, motivation imagery, relaxation imagery and time projection imagery.

Compassion focused imagery

In our experience developing a stance of self-compassion can be difficult for people. Many of the individuals we have seen for therapy and coaching are more likely to be self-critical and show greater compassion towards their colleagues or friends than towards themselves. Often despite evidence to the contrary, individuals berate themselves because, for example, they believe erroneously that in doing so they a) are not letting their standards slip, b) are developing their resilience, or c) do not deserve compassion.

The two-stage process involves visualizing yourself receiving compassion from an external source such as another person and then allowing yourself to feel that you are the recipient of that compassion. To illustrate the application of this process, the coaching transcript below highlights how Petra learned to apply self-compassion after what she described 'a really rubbish client telephone conference'.

Coach:	So in your mind the conference call went badly?
Petra:	Yes I could have said so much more, I could have explained about the new system in more detail. I really didn't sell it at all. I was rubbish.
Coach:	Your manager was also on this conference call; does he agree with your views?
Petra:	Well, he said I did well. We talked about the teleconference afterwards, he said I was really good but then he would as he wants me to get involved in more conference calls.
Coach:	Does he usually give you good feedback?
Petra:	Yes he does at times but I never believe him.
Coach:	So he praised your performance, but you don't believe him, and it seems that this is not the first time that you have rejected his positive feedback. Tell me, would you also encourage the other members of your team not to take on board his positive feedback as you are now doing for yourself?
Petra:	Of course not, he doesn't give praise easily.
Coach:	So it seems that you have one rule for you and one for your colleagues. Others can take positive feedback on board but you don't allow yourself to? Isn't this double standards?
Petra:	Well, yes it is.
Coach:	Can you justify this? Is it OK to treat yourself differently to others?
Petra:	Well no, in theory it isn't right, but it's hard to remember to be kind to myself. It doesn't feel right.
Coach:	Yes it can take practice and time to be kind to yourself, you may want to tell yourself, 'I need to be kind and compassionate towards myself, I need to treat myself as I would others.' Also self-compassion imagery may help reinforce that. Go back to the time when you were sitting with your manager in the

meeting room, close your eyes and picture the scene in as much detail as you can, tell me what your manager said.

Petra: He said that I did really well, I engaged with the clients, went into detail about the system and that the clients seemed really satisfied with my responses.

Coach: OK great, remind yourself of his praise again, allow yourself to feel good and the next time you get praised at work, remember that compassion and visualize yourself feeling it, visualize it enveloping you.

Coping imagery

Coping imagery is a valuable tool which can be used to manage daunting future events, for example events which may be perceived as challenging, such as talking to a manager, giving a presentation and going for an interview. This strategy can help to reduce the pressure often associated with difficult events and improve self-confidence.

The aim of this strategy is to visualize yourself coping adequately – not perfectly – in testing scenarios, because seeing yourself coping perfectly only adds to stress, not reduces it. The process involves four steps outlined below and there is a blank form for you to use in Appendix B.

Example

Dawn was suffering from stress during an organizational reshuffle and was asked to reapply for her current job. This involved being re-interviewed for her post and just the thought of going for an interview (which she hadn't done for 10 years) made her feel stressed. She used the coping imagery form to restructure her thinking about the interview and to manage the interview in her mind's eye. Her completed imagery form is outlined below:

Step 1: Outline the situation that you imagine you will find difficult to manage:
'Re-interviewing for my current job.'

Step 2: Outline the critical aspects of the situation which you find difficult:
'The formality of the interview. I'm most worried about appearing nervous in front of my manager and the other interviewers, about making a complete fool of myself.'

Step 3: Consider the strategies you need to manage this situation adequately.

Having discussed the techniques available to her, Dawn agreed on the following:

'Do some breathing exercises before the interview, remember that I have been doing this job for 10 years, so no-one knows the work better than I do. Remember to drop my shoulders when I am in the interview and be confident.'

Step 4: Visualize yourself coping with the situation using the strategies outlined above.

'Dawn visualized herself going into the interview dressed in her suit, shaking hands with the interviewers, then sitting down, dropping her shoulders and answering the questions with confidence whilst remembering she is the expert in this area. She practised this visualization every day for two weeks before the interview.'

Although she still felt quite nervous during the interview, Dawn found that the practice paid off. She was informed by her manager two weeks after the interview that she was able to stay in her current post.

Letting go of strong emotions

If you are experiencing a strong emotional reaction about a past event or a possible future event which you perceive as emotionally laden (for example a difficult discussion with a colleague or an up-coming work event), consider the event within the context of a calming, serene image. Pick an image which works for you, go back and think of a moment when you felt calm and happy. For example, Maya ruminated on a specific incident during a team building event in which she felt put down by her colleague. She felt extremely angry with her colleague and was finding it hard to let her anger dissipate. In order to facilitate this process she imagined her colleague putting her down while she was sitting on a tranquil beach drinking a margarita. The sense of serenity helped to reduce and to an extent mask her anger. In another example, Clive was not looking forward to a client meeting. He often clashed with this client when talking about contracts and this client had a tendency to rub him up the wrong way. As a result he felt frustrated and angry. To cope with this meeting, Clive imagined talking to the client about the contract whilst sitting on his newly mowed lawn drinking a beer.

Motivation imagery

Motivation imagery is used to assist individuals in motivating themselves into action; it's a simple three-step process with effective results. First think about an area in your life that you want to improve – this can be changing your job or being more assertive. Then consider the steps:

- Step 1: Imagine yourself not making these changes. Think of the impact this may have in your personal and/or professional life, and the effect on those close to you. Then imagine the effect this will have on you and others over the coming years. Try to fully immerse yourself in these outcomes.

- Step 2: Now see yourself having made the changes you considered. What are the outcomes? What is the impact on you and others? How does making these changes benefit your life? How will your life be different?

- Step 3: Now think about how you will make these changes.

Refining choices

If you are making a difficult choice, whether it's professional or personal, imagine yourself as an older adult. See yourself looking back over your whole life. What do you consider consequential or inconsequential now as an older adult? Use this information to guide your current decision making.

Relaxation imagery

Relaxation imagery can be used to relax both your mind and body. A quick relaxation script which if used regularly can induce a more relaxed state is outlined below:

1 Find a place where you won't be disturbed, one which isn't too noisy.

2 Sit down in a comfortable position or lie down.

3 Close your eyes and imagine your favourite place, one which is relaxing and soothing.

4 Concentrate fully on the colours in this place.

5 Concentrate fully on one colour.

6 Concentrate on the sounds in your favourite place.

7 Imagine touching something in your favourite place.

8 Concentrate on the aromas in your favourite place.

Fully immerse yourself in this image and then when you are ready, open your eyes.

Multimodal relaxation method

Another longer relaxation script, known as the 'multimodal relaxation method', covers sensations, imagery and thinking domains, and is outlined below. This can be used to reduce stress and anxiety, physical tension and enhance physiological control such as reducing heart rate or blood pressure. To increase effectiveness it's best used regularly in a quiet environment, such as once a day over a period of two weeks and then less regularly if necessary – and preferably at the same time. Because initially it needs to be read out, it may be helpful to record it yourself onto a digital recorder, computer or mobile phone. An alternative is to ask a family member or friend to read it whist you record it. With practice many people can remember the words and say it themselves either aloud or in their mind.

There are two types of 'pauses' in the script: a 'pause' is about 4 seconds while a 'long pause' is about 15 seconds. As part of the instructions involve looking upwards, it is best to remove contact lenses or miss that section out.

Multimodal relaxation method

Start

Begin by sitting comfortably on a chair and close your eyes. If at any time during the exercise you feel any odd feelings such as tingling sensations, light-headedness or whatever, this is quite normal. If you open your eyes then these feelings will go away. If you carry on with the exercise usually these feelings will disappear anyway.

Listen to the noises outside the room first of all
Long pause
And now listen to the noises inside the room
Pause
You may be aware of yourself breathing
These noises will come and go throughout this session and you can choose to let them just drift over your mind or ignore them if you wish
Pause
Now keeping your eyelids closed and without moving your head, I would like you to look upwards. With your eyes closed, just look upwards
Long pause
Notice the feeling of tiredness
Pause
And relaxation
Pause
In your eye muscles
Pause
Now let your eyes drop back down
Pause
Notice the tiredness and relaxation in those muscles of your eyes
Pause
Let the feeling now travel down your face to your jaw, just relax your jaw
Long pause
Now relax your tongue
Pause
Let the feeling of relaxation slowly travel up over your face to the top of your head
Pause
To the back of your head
Long pause
Then slowly down through your neck muscles
Pause
And down to your shoulders
Long pause
Now concentrate on relaxing your shoulders, just let them drop down

Pause

Now let that feeling of relaxation now in your shoulders slowly travel down your right arm, down through the muscles, down through your elbow, down through your wrist, to your hand, right down to your finger tips

Long pause

Let the feeling of relaxation now in your shoulders slowly travel down your left arm, down through your muscles, down through your elbow, through your wrist, down to your hand, right down to your finger tips

Long pause

And let that feeling of relaxation now in your shoulders slowly travel down your chest right down to your stomach

Pause

Just concentrate on your breathing

Pause

Notice that every time you breathe out you feel more

Pause

And more relaxed

Long pause

Let the feeling of relaxation travel down from your shoulders right down your back

Long pause

Right down your right leg, down through the muscles, through your knee, down through your ankle

Pause

To your foot, right down to your toes

Long pause

Let the feeling of relaxation now travel down your left leg

Pause

Down through the muscles, down through your knee, down through your ankle

Pause

To your foot, right down to your toes

Long pause

I'll give you a few moments now

Pause

To allow you to concentrate on any part of your body that you would like to relax further

15-second pause minimum

I want you to concentrate on your breathing again

Pause

Notice as you breathe

Pause

On each out-breath you feel more and more relaxed

Long pause

I would like you in your mind to say a number of your choice such as the number one

Pause (NB If the number evokes an emotion in you choose another number)

And say it every time you breathe out

Long pause
This will help you to push away any unwanted thoughts you may have
Pause
Each time you breathe out just say the number in your mind
30-second pause
I want you now
Pause
To think of your favourite relaxing place
Long pause
Try and see it in your mind's eye
Long pause
Look at the colours
Pause
Now focus on one colour
Pause
Now concentrate on any sounds or noises in your favourite relaxing place.
If there are no sounds, then focus on the silence
Long pause
Now concentrate on any smells or aromas in your favourite relaxing place
Long pause
Now just imagine touching something
Pause
In your favourite relaxing place
Long pause
Just imagine how it feels
Long pause
I want you now to concentrate on your breathing again
Pause
Notice once again that every time you breathe out
Pause
You feel more
Pause
And more relaxed
Long pause
Whenever you want to in the future you will be able to remember your
favourite place or the breathing exercise and it will help you to relax quickly
Long pause
In a few moments' time, but not quite yet, I'm going to count to three
Pause
And you will be able to open your eyes in your own time
Pause
One
Pause
Two
Pause
Three

© Stephen Palmer 1993

Time projection imagery

Essentially, time projection imagery involves thinking about a current stressful problem and then asking yourself if you would view the same situation as stressful in seven days' time, two weeks' time, four weeks' time, six months' time, one and two years' time. The aim is to recognize that current events can be blown out of proportion and with time, a person regains perspective. Also, if you are not still thinking about an event in the future it may not be worth getting upset about in the present. Essentially this technique is used to take the 'angst' out of situations.

Dan used time projection to address an image of a meeting he attended in his workplace. During the meeting he raised his voice at one of the company directors. This led to a heated exchange which although resolved made him 'feel quite sick' every time he recalled the meeting. He worried about bumping into the director in the office and that she would never forget his comments. Using time projection Dan was able to recognize that even though in two days' time he may still be thinking about the meeting, as time progressed and certainly in one week's time he would have forgotten the experience. Therefore on that basis it was not worth getting stressed about. Also Dan considered the director's position and asked himself, 'Considering that the situation was resolved, would the director still be thinking about the event even though it happened one week ago? Would the director not have other issues to think about rather than our exchange?'

Chapter Five
Understanding and managing anxiety, panic and phobias

In this chapter we focus on understanding anxiety, panic and phobias. The chapter is divided into three parts, with the initial emphasis on anxiety: what it is, the signs of anxiety, how it is maintained and the techniques applied to control it. We then focus on how to manage panic before going on to address how to cope with phobias.

What is anxiety?

Anxiety is a normal reaction in certain situations. It is part of the fight or flight response: for example, feeling anxious when confronted by an intruder or when involved in an accident is normal. Anxiety only becomes problematic when it occurs in a situation which is not normally considered to be anxiety provoking and it hinders functioning at the time: for example if your heart races, your mouth is dry and you feel faint during a video conference and you have to walk out of the room with your colleagues watching you, or if this happens whilst you are participating in a seminar.

Worrying often goes hand in hand with anxiety, as individuals often worry about experiencing anxiety – as does stress. Panic can also be seen as a more extreme form of anxiety. One way of visualizing the link between the three is to use a continuum:

Stress   Anxiety   Panic

Increased levels of stress can often lead to anxiety and individuals experiencing anxiety can also have symptoms of panic. Worrying is generally seen to be a component of all three, although individuals can be prone to worrying without experiencing the full quota of anxiety symptoms.

What constitutes anxiety?

Any or all of the following:

- **Physiological or physical symptoms include**: tightness in the chest, a lump in your throat, difficulty breathing, muscle tension, heart racing, shaking, trembling, feeling dizzy, feeling faint, problems swallowing, sweating, dry mouth, feeling nauseous, churning stomach, restlessness and needing to urinate frequently.

- **Cognitive symptoms include**: negative thoughts such as, 'I'm going to look stupid, I can't cope, I've made a fool of myself and they must think I'm an idiot.'

- **Behavioural responses include**: avoiding the situation if possible, increased use of alcohol, taking over-the-counter remedies or prescribed medication to manage the symptoms.

Most people experience a selection of the above symptoms when thinking or encountering their anxiety provoking situation.

Anxiety can be experienced in different guises, for example:

- **Social anxiety**: some individuals experience social anxiety, which is a fear of acting in a way which is perceived as being embarrassing whether in a work or social context. Common experiences include feeling socially anxious when with colleagues or friends in a restaurant or a pub or other social situations, and a fear and experience of blushing when with other people.

● **Agoraphobia:** is a fear of being in a situation which the person perceives they cannot escape from. They worry about making a 'fool of themselves', 'doing something stupid' such as fainting or 'losing control'. In its extreme form it can affect individuals to such an extent that they struggle to leave their home; eventually they can even become housebound. The situations in which individuals feel symptoms of agoraphobia include: queues; public transport; driving on motorways; lifts; traffic jams; supermarkets; bridges; cinemas and large crowds (such as at concerts). It is considered to be a complex phobia as it can involve a number of feared situations. However, if the fear and subsequent avoidance only occurs in one specific situation – for example, travelling on trains – then it may be a specific phobia instead.

● **Generalized anxiety disorder:** known as GAD, this can affect up to 5 per cent of the population. A key feature of GAD is a tendency towards excessive worrying, combined with irritability, concentration problems, tension and poor sleep.

● **Health anxiety:** also commonly known as hypochondriasis, this is a preoccupation or excessive worry about your health, which can include having a fear of cancer, a brain tumour or other life-threatening diseases.

● **Obsessive–compulsive disorder:** is characterized by having thoughts (obsessions) which are intrusive or unacceptable and impulses (compulsions) which are repetitive and often carried out in a stereotypical manner. For example, we have found that when anxious some individuals develop the tendency to check that their e-mails were sent to the correct person, or check that they shut down their computer correctly or check to make sure they have not made any mistakes in the reports or e-mails they have written. They don't just check once or twice but again and again in order to prevent any problems. Other repetitive checking behaviours include checking the front door is shut and checking that electrical equipment is unplugged and that taps are turned off.

Anxiety is also a component of other problems such as anger, depression or bullying, all of which are also described in this book.

The causes of anxiety

The causes of anxiety vary and below are some of the main reasons cited for anxiety:

- **Genetic predisposition:** there is research to suggest that anxiety can run in families, so if either your mother or father or close relatives have suffered from anxiety, it is possible that you are genetically predisposed to react in an anxious manner, especially when under pressure.

- **Learned behaviour:** anxiety can also be learnt from significant others. If one of your parents is scared of spiders then you may have learnt that spiders are threatening. In the same vein if one of your parents worries a lot and was over-protective when you were a child, it is possible that as an adult you now worry more than you need to because you learnt from them to worry.

- **Stressful life events:** can contribute to the increased chances of developing anxiety; these can be a combination of work and personal events. For example Michelle described going through a difficult divorce which she was able to cope with until she began to experience prolonged pressure at work, which included working long hours over a period of months and a difficult relationship with her manager. Together the pressure at work and home led to anxiety and then panic attacks.

- **Drugs:** prescribed or recreational drugs can contribute to the onset of anxiety and panic. Likewise regular consumption of strong coffee can trigger anxiety, in particular an increased heart rate.

What can maintain anxiety?

Two key factors serve to maintain anxiety. The first is avoidance and the second is adopting safety behaviours. Generally, avoidance breeds further avoidance and leaves you feeling stuck, while safety behaviours are actions employed by individuals to keep their anxiety to a minimum. For example, keeping your head down and avoiding eye contact during meetings to ensure you don't get asked questions or giving short answers to questions and not engaging fully in conversations in case you may say the wrong thing. Although avoiding situations which make you feel anxious and using safety behaviours to reduce the chances of feeling anxious are understandable reactions, in reality they are not helpful. They function to maintain your anxiety, to stop you coping with the anxiety in the present and in the future in a constructive manner.

For example, take Ishmael who had a fear of standing up and talking in front of people. Once, when talking about a new project to a group of five other employees a number of months ago, he struggled to answer a question and he felt himself go red and feared that he was swaying while standing on the spot. He put the experience down to too much coffee and tiredness. However he started to feel anxious when he was in meetings, specifically meetings in which he had to talk about project development and answer questions. Then he began to feel anxious before the meetings, while in meetings he felt that his face was always red, his chest felt tight and he felt dizzy. He started to dread meetings and as a result he went out of his way to avoid going to any meetings in which he was expected to contribute. He even applied for new jobs as a way of managing his anxiety.

In a second example, Emma experienced symptoms of anxiety in her office environment; she described herself as quite shy, as someone who found it hard to fit in with others. She had recently moved into an open plan-office where the other employees seemed to know each other well. They laughed a lot, sharing the same sense of humour and went out together for lunch, often talking about where they went the previous evening. Emma found it hard to fit in.

She believed that they didn't seem at all interested in her or what she had to say and appeared to ignore her and chat amongst themselves. She started to feel anxious when going in to work and during the day; she wanted to look as if she didn't care about their behaviour. She tried not to talk to her team other than the standard 'hello' in the morning, just in case she said the wrong thing, and she worked hard at 'appearing busy', keeping her head down reading work manuals or focusing on the computer screen.

How to manage anxiety

To manage anxiety, you can employ a range of different strategies. Here we start by focusing on addressing anticipatory anxiety or anticipating that you will be anxious (which in turn can become a self-fulfilling prophecy) and then how to deconstruct anxiety-focused thinking.

Anticipatory anxiety

Anticipating how anxiety provoking situations will be is a common feature of general anxiety. If you recognize that you experience anticipatory anxiety ask yourself: 'How does the anxiety I am feeling right now help me deal with the situation? Does it aid or hinder my progress?'

If you recognize that it only serves to hinder your progress, then consider what you can do to manage it: for example use relaxation techniques or remind yourself in a calm manner that it's unhelpful and focus instead on the task in hand.

If on the other hand you see some benefits in anticipating the worst when it comes to the situation, consider testing the validity of your concerns using the automatic negative thought form. An example of Ishmael's anticipatory thoughts about standing up in meetings is shown in Table 5.1.

TABLE 5.1   Example of Ishmael's automatic thought record form

Situation A	Your negative thoughts about the situation (A) B	Your feelings and physical responses C	Develop realistic thoughts D	Effective new way of dealing with the situation E
Thinking about talking during a meeting	I'll go red Then I'll look incompetent What if when standing up I start to sway? They'll all laugh at me or think I'm weak	Feel anxious, Butterflies in my stomach My chest feels tight	Even if I do go red, and I'm not sure that I will, I can cope. I've seem many people go red and I haven't immediately jumped to the conclusion that they are weak Nobody has said anything about me swaying. Surely they would have pointed this out if this was the case?	Don't jump ahead; recognize that I don't know how meetings will go. I can cope and I do have the knowledge to answer questions.

Deconstructing negative automatic thoughts

Work through your anxiety-provoking negative automatic thoughts with the automatic thought form using the Socratic questions outlined in Chapter 2. An example of Emma's automatic thought form is shown in Table 5.2.

TABLE 5.2 Example of Emma's automatic thought record form

Situation A	Your negative thoughts about the situation (A) B	Your feelings and physical responses C	Develop realistic thoughts D	Effective new way of dealing with the situation E
Talking to David and Paula about my weekend	They look really bored They are not interested I'm running out of things to say	Anxiety Feel as if my throat is closing up	How do I know that they were bored and not interested? Where is my proof? They were just listening to what I said as they do to others in the office I focused on what is wrong with the conversation as opposed what is right I said what I wanted to say and then Paula talked about her weekend: that is normal	Talk to people in the office about their weekends, the weather and work. Practise doing this It's not my job to keep conversations going as then they become one sided It's OK to have silences and just go with the flow

Calming words or images

Repeating a word you find calming or remembering an image from your past which is associated with happiness and serenity can be effective. For example, Ishmael repeated the word 'calm' to himself, while Emma repeated the word 'picture' that brought to mind a painting her son had done in school, which made her feel content.

If you use this technique try to keep to only one word and one image, otherwise it is easy to get confused. If you focus on remembering a pleasant image, aim to practise remembering the image in as much detail as possible outside the anxiety-provoking situations, so that when you are anxious you are focusing on an image you know well and not one you need to hastily construct at the time.

Addressing safety behaviours

As mentioned above, safety behaviours inhibit dealing with anxiety; if you continue to use safety behaviours your anxiety will remain. To address these behaviours aim to isolate and eradicate them. Try to act differently to test out the assumption that safety behaviours work.

In the case of Emma (who felt anxious in the office) she made the effort to speak to other people and look around when sitting at her desk to make eye contact. The results were positive and she felt motivated to address the rest of the safety behaviours and her anxiety (see Table 5.3).

TABLE 5.3   Example of Emma's safety behaviours

My safety behaviours in order of priority	Actions to reduce the behaviours	Results
• Avoid eye contact	Make an effort to speak to one person every day	I managed to have a short conversation every time and people seemed friendly enough
• Appearing busy at my computer	Looking round a couple of times a day	I found that if someone was doing the same they smiled at me or even said something to me
• Holding onto pencils or pens when speaking to others just in case my hands shake	Stop doing that to see if hands do shake	Found that initially my hands did shake but nobody seemed to notice and the more I did it, the less my hands shook

Relaxation strategies

Relaxation reduces tension which can build up quickly during periods of anxiety. The relaxation strategies outlined in the Chapter 4, if applied regularly in conjunction with the other strategies outlined in this chapter, can lead to a reduction in symptoms.

Breathing strategies

The components of anxiety, and panic in particular, often include difficulties with breathing, such as shallow, quick or deep breathing. Known as over-breathing or hyperventilation this occurs as a result of a drop in the level of carbon dioxide in the blood, which contributes to an increase in the PH level, leading to symptoms such as dizziness, difficulty breathing, trembling, tingling, blurred vision and muscle tension notably in the chest. These symptoms are produced by the body to regulate the oxygen and carbon dioxide in the blood and are misinterpreted as unsafe, which they are not; rather it's the individual's catastrophic interpretation of the symptoms that can lead to an escalation of anxiety and panic symptoms.

For example, Derek was under pressure at work due to the re-organization of his marketing department at work. He was working longer hours and was concerned about the impact of the reorganization on both his and the team's roles. After three months of working under pressure he noticed that his heart was beginning to race and that his palms were sweaty and he had a tightness in his chest. He began to worry and thought that it was a heart problem so saw his GP, who after examining him, said that he was suffering from anxiety and panic attacks. While Derek felt to an extent reassured by the GP's comments he was concerned that the GP had missed something and that he was indeed physically ill. In addition he began to feel out of breath in the morning rush hour on the tube and in the office, and had mental pictures of himself lying on the floor in the office unable to breathe and an ambulance being called. After seeing a cardiologist, who also diagnosed anxiety and panic, he referred himself to a psychologist, who explained to him about the spiral of anxiety and panic and how the symptoms can be misinterpreted, which in turn maintains the symptoms of panic and anxiety (see Figure 5.1).

FIGURE 5.1 Derek's anxiety spiral

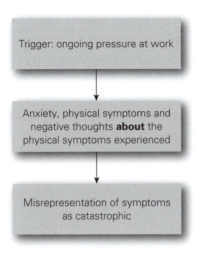

In order to manage these symptoms of over-breathing you need to bring your breathing under control. To do this a technique called breathing retraining can be used. The steps outlined below provide a cohesive summary of the process:

- First, you need to ensure that you are breathing from your stomach not your chest. To do this correctly, in a sitting or lying down position, place your hand on your stomach and watch your hand go up and down. It is important that you breathe from your stomach or diaphragm not your chest.

- Then practise breathing in and out through your nose; you are aiming for about 10–12 breaths a minute.

- Aim to practise this technique for 10 minutes twice a day for at least one week. Once you feel that you are competent in using this strategy you can reduce the number of times you practise it. However, it is important to keep practising breathing retraining, especially when you are not anxious or feeling panicky in order to get the technique right, so when you experience the symptoms you can quickly and proficiently use the strategy without trying to remember how it works.

What is panic?

As we mentioned at the beginning of this chapter, experiencing panic or having a panic attack is a common feature of anxiety. About 1 in 100 adults in Britain have a panic disorder. Panic attacks can also be experienced independently of anxiety, and often Accident and Emergency departments are the initial port of call for individuals who experience their first panic symptoms. This is because the symptoms of panic such as palpitations and chest pain coupled with extreme fear can easily be interpreted as signs of a heart attack. For some people the diagnosis of panic can be a welcome relief as they have a name for their collective symptoms; while others, despite receiving the all clear from a doctor, find it hard to accept that their symptoms are due to panic as opposed to physical problems such as heart problems or even a stroke.

Panic attacks usually occur out of the blue, especially during or after periods of prolonged stress. They are often associated with specific situations such as being stuck in the tube during the rush hour, crowded supermarkets or in the car while on a motorway. In these cases panic attacks can turn into phobias. They can also occur at night whilst asleep.

As panic attacks invoke a strong sense of fear, individuals start to worry about having another panic attack; this anticipatory anxiety serves to maintain the fear. In addition having experienced a panic attack in a specific context, individuals can start to avoid these situations and other similar situations which they believe may trigger another attack. Often they develop an increased sensitivity to bodily sensations which they believe can lead to the onset of an attack.

What are the symptoms of panic?

- A racing heart and palpitations
- Discomfort in the chest or pain
- Sweating
- Nausea

Example

Mark suffered with palpitations, chest pain, sweating and nausea following a difficult experience on the tube. He described being in a packed tube at the height of the rush hour; he was standing when the train stopped at a red signal. The train driver announced that they would be stuck for the next 10 minutes and with that he began to feel hot and uncomfortable. His heart starting to race, he felt lightheaded and faint and started to sweat. Looking around he begun to worry about what the other people on the tube were thinking of him and he desperately wanted to get off, which he did at the next stop. Once he stepped out of the station his symptoms abated and he was able to continue his journey into work on the bus.

Following a check-up from the doctor – who said that he had experienced a panic attack – he went back on the tube that evening. However, he was feeling anxious about it and found that he felt faint yet again standing on the platform. Once again his heart started to race. Over the next week or so he found that the symptoms came and went and seemed worse when the train was overly packed. He also found that one Saturday following an evening out he began to experience the same symptoms while stuck in a traffic jam. To cope with his symptoms he tried to avoid driving at peak times over the weekend and he began to leave home later to avoid the rush hour. Over a period of three months this behaviour impacted negatively on his role as he was missing morning meetings. It was at this point that he was asked to speak to HR. Having explained his symptoms, he was referred for cognitive behaviour therapy to manage his panic.

- Tingling or numbness
- Feeling dizzy, light-headed or feeling faint
- A sense of unreality or feeling detached from yourself (a common feature is the sense of looking down on your body from above)
- Sensation of choking
- Fear of dying, losing control or going mad

As with anxiety, the experience of panic is a combination of physiological symptoms (eg sweating, fear), behavioural symptoms (most commonly avoidance) and self-hindering thinking styles which often involve the misinterpretation of symptoms, for example thinking 'I'm out of control', or 'I'm going to die.'

The causes of panic

As with anxiety the reasons for having a panic attack vary. Current research suggests that there is some evidence that panic can run in families, and substance misuse or increased consumption of caffeine can lead to panic as can a build-up of life events (such as change in job or relationship problems often combined with increased pressure levels).

How can we manage panic?

Many of the techniques described above apply both to anxiety and panic management: the key to controlling your panic is to understand it. Remember, as uncomfortable as panic symptoms can be, they are not dangerous; your panic will peak and then fade. Panic attacks do not go on forever, typically lasting about 10 minutes, and people do not die from panic attacks. Neither do people usually faint during panic attacks, as in order to faint, blood pressure needs to be low rather than high, which it generally is during panic attacks.

Some of the more common beliefs associated with panic are listed below. If they seem familiar to you then work through them using the strategies outlined Chapter 2, covering unhelpful thinking patterns. Specifically use the automatic thought form and a blank copy, specifically adapted to dealing with panic, which is available in Appendix C. A form completed by Neil, who experienced panic when walking across a packed trading floor, is seen in Table 5.4.

TABLE 5.4   Neil's completed panic management form

Situation/ trigger	Your response to the situation (eg heart racing, dizziness, feeling faint)	Your negative thoughts about your response	Your realistic thoughts
Walking across the trading floor	Feeling light headed Hands feeling sweaty Need to hold onto someone's desk	I'm going to faint Everyone will notice; how embarrassing	These are just symptoms of panic, they will go I haven't fainted before and there is no reason that I will now

The NATs linked to panic are as follows:

- I'm going mad.
- My chest pain means that I'm going to have a heart attack.
- I'm out of control.
- I'm dying.
- I can't breathe.
- Something awful is happening to me.
- I can't stand it.
- I have to get out.
- I feel so dizzy.
- I'm going to faint.
- I'm choking.
- Everyone is looking at me.

In addition to using the automatic thought form, some of the key strategies used to reduce and eliminate panic are breathing strategies and a reduction in safety behaviors. To illustrate how to apply these strategies, therapeutic interventions are outlined below.

Case example: working with panic

Following an assessment of Mark's problems and a discussion about the rationale behind cognitive behavioural therapy, the therapist drew a diagram which outlined the development and the maintenance of his panic symptoms. Mark was able to recognize that while he originally thought that the panic attacks occurred out of the blue, his lack of sleep together with work problems contributed to the development of his symptoms, which in essence were maintained by lack of knowledge of panic and a tendency to avoid getting on the tube during rush hour and later driving during peak hours. Once Mark understood that panic was only a set of symptoms (in this case triggered by poor breathing techniques) his confidence in tackling his symptoms increased. Mark also found it helpful to learn that although he felt light headed and faint during the panic attacks, he was unlikely to faint. Over the course of the therapy, Mark practisced the breathing strategies he needed to manage his symptoms and used an automatic thought form to address his panic-related beliefs.

The therapist and Mark then addressed his avoidance behaviours (ie not getting on the tube at rush hour and not driving at peak hours). It was agreed that Mark would start by driving during the weekend peak hours again to improve his confidence. Once he was able to do that without feeling panicky, he went back to getting on the rush hour trains on an everyday basis. Although initially he found this difficult and still experienced some symptoms, he was able to stay on the tube for the whole journey without getting off at an earlier station. The therapist also encouraged Mark to develop a coping card on which he wrote some of the key principles related to panic he had learnt during the course of the therapy. A copy of Mark coping card is shown below.

Mark's coping strategies:

> This is only panic, it will peak and then fade.
>
> I can manage it; I have done so until now.
>
> I'm not going to faint because my pulse is racing.
>
> I'm not going mad; this is just my body reacting to anxiety, which although uncomfortable is harmless.
>
> It will pass as it has done.
>
> I can stick it out again.
>
> I've done it, it wasn't that bad, so I deserve a reward.

In addition Mark cut down on his consumption of alcohol, as he found that after a couple of pints the night before the chances of feeling some panic the next day increased. Then over the course of two sessions the therapy focused on stress management strategies to manage his overall stress levels.

Phobias

The term 'phobia' comes from the Greek meaning 'flight' or 'terror'. Knowing someone with a phobia or having a phobia yourself is familiar to everyone. Some of the more common phobias include agoraphobia, which is described above, claustrophobia, spider phobia (arachnophobia) and a fear of flying known as aviopobia.

Treating phobias

The most effective form of treatment for phobias is known as 'in-vivo exposure', that is facing your fear step by step, starting with the least anxiety-provoking situation. So if you have a fear of dogs, you might start with watching a programme about dogs before going on to being in a room with a dog and its owner and then gradually getting closer to the dog and stroking it, whilst reminding yourself that dogs are lovely animals that rarely bite unless provoked. In practice this is more difficult with certain phobias such as a fear of flying, so for this phobia a combination of imaginal exposure together with in vivo exposures is recommended. Imaginal exposure involves clearly imagining in your mind's eye, in as much detail as possible, the situation or object that is causing you anxiety.

Case example 1: aviophobia

Martin, a deputy director of a geological company, developed a fear of flying after experiencing severe turbulence on one of his regular business flights. He suddenly felt vulnerable and began to consider the chances of a plane crash. As a result he began to worry about flying at least three days before the flight, he always checked his will before the flight to make sure all his affairs were in order, and he drank alcohol on the plane to reduce his anxiety. Once on the plane, Martin's heart raced, he was worried about having a heart attack, the pilot being incompetent and the plane crashing.

To manage his fears Martin reminded himself that a racing heart is a sign of anxiety not a heart attack, and that thoughts don't equal facts (ie just because he thought the plane could crash doesn't mean it will happen). In fact he reminded himself of the statistics about flying which point to the fact that flying is very safe and that 'the chances of winning the lottery are higher than the chances of the plane crashing'. Martin also applied daily relaxation techniques four weeks before his next flight to reduce his physical symptoms and used coping imagery every second day to see himself coping well during the flight without drinking excessive amounts of alcohol.

Case example 2: fear of lifts

Marianna worked on the eighth floor and regularly used the lift without feeling any fear until her friend described being stuck in a lift with eight others for over an hour. Then by chance three weeks after this incident Marianna watched a horror film which included a scene in which the lift plunged to the ground killing everyone in it. Marianna then begun to worry about 'something bad happening in the lift', and while standing in the lift she experienced some anxiety symptoms and begun to 'feel stuck'. While she recognized the fear was irrational, she was surprised about the strength of her fear and 'how quickly it crept up on her'. To manage her anxiety Marianna reverted to using the stairs. While on the plus side she described feeling fitter, on the negative side her role involved going to reception on the ground floor and accompanying individuals coming for interviews to the interviewing suite. She began to dread coming up with interviewees in the lift and was worried that they would see that she looked white and was shaking while in the lift with them. To manage her phobia Marianna made a list of lift-related steps that she would undertake gradually to reduce her fear. Starting with the easiest step, she made herself a promise to tackle one step every day. Her list of tasks is outlined below:

- Go up from the ground floor in the lift to the second floor with a colleague (Sue who knows how I feel about lifts) when it's not crowded, twice a day.

- Go up and down from the ground floor in the lift to the fifth floor when it's not crowded twice a day on my own.

- Go up and down in the lift to the eighth floor when it's not crowded four times a day.

- Go up in the lift when arriving in the morning with everyone else and then down with everyone else and keep doing this regardless of whether I feel a bit anxious.

- Remember – keep going don't stop, don't bottle out.

By confronting her fear, using breathing exercises and reminding herself that there is nothing to worry about and that lifts are safe (otherwise why wasn't everyone scared of using lifts?) Marianna managed to control her anxiety and after a couple of weeks she noticed that her level of anxiety was much lower than previously experienced.

Chapter Six
Dealing with worry

In this chapter we address the ubiquitous issue of worry. It is an altogether common experience as we all worry at times about various issues such as health (our own health and that of others), work, relationships, family issues and more recently the state of the economy and terrorist threats.

Tallis *et al* (1994) found that on average, individuals worry most days and that a worry episode can last for 1–30 minutes. While this is not unusual, worry can become troublesome when it is excessive (ie you recognize that you worry a lot and may think it's a good idea to carry on worrying). Some individuals report 'feeling worried all day' and can often having trouble falling asleep because they are worrying or 'overthinking'. This can be about what has happened earlier during the day or what may happen in the future. Worrying is also often associated with other psychological issues such anxiety and depression.

If you recognize that you are a worrier and that it impacts on your day-to-day functioning, it is important that you read and work through this chapter. First we focus on what constitutes worrying, its impact on our psychological health and how worry can lead to even more worry. We then address the cognitive and behavioural strategies you can use to manage worrying.

What is worry?

Worries are predominantly unhelpful thoughts and images, and often one worry leads very quickly to another. This process can cause a downward spiral and a negative and rapid impact on your mood. Worry can leave you feeling mentally exhausted, anxious or apprehensive. It's like a runaway overloaded cargo train heading for a crash, the cargo being all the accumulated worries which are spilling over the side of the containers. Worry can often breed worry and individuals often end up worrying about being worried. Commonly individuals ruminate about past, current and future events. For example, worrying about what you could have done or said differently; about what is happening in your life right now; and then about future events. Often the last takes the form of dwelling on the worst possible scenario. So worrying can be seen as a form of catastrophizing – that is, imagining the most damaging outcome.

For example, take Chen who was worried about speaking to his line manager about his promotion. His negative spiral of worry went like this:

'If I don't get the promotion it probably means he thinks I'm not up to the job.'

'It will get around the department and soon everyone will know I messed up.'

'What is my wife going to say, as we really need the extra cash?'

'We won't have the money to pay for the extension, so the baby will need to sleep in our bedroom.'

'That will be awful. We'll start to row again; it will be like the last time we were under so much pressure.'

'We'll probably end up separating and I'll have to live with my parents; what a nightmare!'

At the beginning of this spiral Chen was a little concerned about his promotion, but by the time he reached the end of the spiral he was feeling miserable and reluctant to see his manager to talk about the promotion. He viewed the discussion with his manager as a negative event with possible catastrophic consequences.

The impact of worry

As we have mentioned already, individuals who worry can also feel anxious and low. In addition, worry can be associated with stress, physical problems such as headaches, colds and insomnia, an overall decrease in life satisfaction and traits such as a pessimistic attitude, perfectionism and a lack of belief in our own abilities to problem solve.

Why is it then that people still worry?

In our experience (which is substantiated by the research into worrying), many individuals often cite a list of ostensible benefits of worrying. They can convince themselves that worrying is actually helpful. Some of the more common arguments are as below:

- If I worry about the event it's less likely to happen.
- Worrying is a way of solving my problems.
- Worrying about an event is a way of ensuring that I'm prepared for it.

In addition individuals who worry about worrying have the following negative views about worrying:

- If I keep on worrying I will go mad.
- I'll never be able to stop worrying.

At face value the initial reasons outlined for worrying seem plausible, but if worrying is advantageous, then everyone would worry, which is not the case. Likewise worrying does not make you feel happy, it does the opposite – it can make you feel tense and stressed. Ultimately worry breeds worry.

In this next section we focus on how to address these not so helpful reasons together with outlining strategies devised to reduce worrying.

Strategies to tackle worrying

One strategy often employed by our clients and coachees is to try and stop worrying. However, this can often have the opposite effect;

the more you try and stop, the more you end up worrying, so thought or image suppression is not necessarily effective. Another strategy regularly used is to 'try and think more positively'. While this can work for a short time, it is not possible to think positively about everything all the time; again it just doesn't work.

Tackling the reasons given for worrying

In the first example, 'If I worry about the event it's less likely to happen', consider how this idea actually works in practice, think about how many times worry has actually reduced the chances of an event happening. If you do come up with some examples, think carefully about any other factors that could have impacted on the event occurring. It's probable that these factors influenced the chances of the event happening and not your thinking. If indeed worrying was such a powerful process with positive consequences then we would all be employing it to reduce the chances of certain events happening.

In the second example, 'Worrying is a way of solving my problems', think about how you feel when you use worry to manage your problems? Does this feeling help you to solve problems or in fact impede this process? In our experience, worrying is associated with anxiety and low mood, both of which do not facilitate problem solving; rather they hinder the problem-solving process. Later in this chapter we discuss an alternative strategy to worrying which is more effective in dealing with problems.

In the third example, 'Worrying about an event is way of ensuring that I'm prepared for it', note that worrying does not prepare you for events. Think about how worrying makes you feel. More than likely it makes you feel anxious. If that is the case how does feeling anxious prepare you for an event? Answer: it doesn't! Do you need to prepare for all events? Maybe a preferable way to get yourself ready for certain events such as giving a speech, a presentation or going for an interview is talking about it with a friend or colleague or using coping imagery, which is outlined in Chapter 4.

How to manage worry about worrying

- In the first example, 'If I keep on worrying I will go mad' ask yourself, how do you know for certain that you will go mad? Do you have any concrete proof that you will go mad? Do you know or know of other people who have gone mad solely as a result of worrying?

- In the second example, 'I'll never be able to stop worrying', how do you know this will happen? Instead of predicting the future, focus on the 'here and now', thinking about how you can manage your worries in a different way.

List the advantages and disadvantages of worrying

One technique used to address the costs and benefits of worrying is to make a list of the advantages and disadvantages of worrying. This is best done in writing: see Table 6.1 for the list that Pauline wrote relating to her worry that that other people don't like her.

TABLE 6.1 Pauline's list of advantages and disadvantages of worrying

Advantages of worrying	Disadvantages of worrying
I can change how I am to ensure everyone likes me	I feel on edge constantly
I feel in control	It won't make any difference as to whether people will like me or not
People will like me	It stops me focusing on what else is going on around me
	Worrying hasn't ensured that everyone likes me until now
	I avoid meeting new people because I worry too much about how they will react to me

The worry form

The worry form is an adapted version of the automatic thought form mentioned already in this book. Use it to make a note of your worries and the impact they have on your feelings and behaviours before using the questions below to reassess your worries. A blank worry form is provided in Appendix D.

To reassess your concerns ask yourself:

- How likely is it that my worry will come true?
- What is the likelihood that my worry won't come true?
- How has worrying about events helped me in the past?
- Right now, how is worrying affecting me?
- Does worry really help me to be in control or is the opposite true, worrying makes me more out of control?
- What are the pros of cons of holding onto my worry?
- Even if the worst happens, would I not be able to manage the situation?
- What would I do to cope?
- What is the probability, based on my past experiences, that the outcome will be neutral or positive?

Worry vs problem solving

As noted earlier, worrying can be erroneously viewed as a way of solving problems, when in fact it hinders the process. Research into worrying has also highlighted that worriers lack self-belief in their problem-solving abilities. In other words, they don't think that they have the skills to know how to manage their problems. Therefore we have found that providing a structured problem-solving format called 'The PRACTICE solutions form' to manage concerns in a more constructive way is an excellent alternative to worrying. Using the form can be empowering. It's an easy tool to apply and increases the chances of a successful outcome.

This seven-step form can be used when a worry needs to be addressed in a practical manner, and a blank PRACTICE solutions form is available in Appendix E.

The key here is to recognize that worrying is a waste of time and it does not provide a solution. If you do have a worry which needs to be addressed then use the form to deal with the worry and then let it go.

Schedule a worry period

Setting aside a time to worry, instead of dwelling on your worries and blowing then out of all proportion, can be helpful. Make a decision to delay worrying until a specific time in the day: for example, decide to worry for 20 minutes in the late afternoon. When worries pop into your head, try to distract yourself. If it helps write down the worry and focus instead on what you are doing at that time. Then during your 'worry period' allow yourself to worry and to problem solve your worries. We have found that using this strategy helps individuals learn that they can control their worrying.

If you find yourself having trouble falling asleep because as soon as your head hits the pillow you start worrying about work or other issues, before you go to bed do the following: make a list of your concerns and transfer the worries from your mind onto paper. If you wake up and start to worry, remind yourself that: a) you have already noted down your worries on paper, so you don't need to keep thinking about the issues right now; and b) that this process is only going to stop you falling back to sleep and make you feel worse in the morning. Don't attempt to solve your worries in the middle of the night; it's a waste of valuable sleeping time.

Managing the tricky 'what if's'

If you recognize yourself using what if's, such as, 'What if I don't achieve my outcomes?', 'What if I can't inspire my team?', 'What if my marketing skills don't meet the standards required?', then aim to stay in the present. Asking what if's can open up a black hole of questions and worries that cannot all be answered. Instead focus on *what is*: that is what you can do right now to control the worry.

Reasons why not to worry

If you are at the stage where you accept that worrying is not productive, consider making a list of the reasons why not to worry. When you have made a list of five or so good points, reread that list at least twice a day for two weeks, in order to remind yourself not to worry. An example of a list follows:

The reasons why I don't need to worry

- Worrying makes me feel stressed.

- Worrying makes me feel anxious.

- When I feel anxious and stressed I can't think properly.

- Worrying doesn't have any productive outcomes.

- Worrying is waste of my precious time.

- Worrying is a dead-end activity.

The proactive approach to managing worrying

Figure 6.1 highlights the actions required to manage worrying. If you cannot change what you are worrying about (eg whether or not you will get a bonus) you can put the worry on a cloud and see it float away or put it in a bottle and let it drift out to sea. Or else consider if there is anything you can do to improve your chances of receiving a bonus and then do it, or make a plan to address it at a later date. (An adapted copy of this figure is available in Appendix F.)

FIGURE 6.1   A proactive approach to worrying

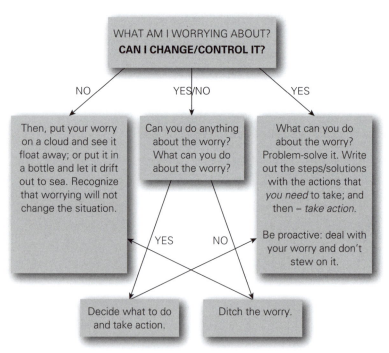

SOURCE: Adapted from Flower Associates International 2010

Dealing with uncertainty

A common factor that underlies worrying is the demand or need for certainty. Worriers want to be in control of their destinies. Well, the only certainty in life is death, other than that there is no certainty. Ask yourself if you can live with uncertainty? How do you cope now with uncertainties such as perhaps the state of the economy or your children's schooling, the unpredictability of your journey into and back from work. If you can cope with current uncertainties you can manage situations when they occur in the future. It's better to focus your energy into the here and now as opposed to imagining a gloomy future. Remind yourself that certainty is not a necessity for anyone. If all our futures were mapped out to our exact specifications our lives would be terribly predictable and boring, without interest or excitement.

Putting it all together

Whether you recognize that you have been a 'worrier' for a long time or have found yourself lapsing into worry frequently, it is important to recognize that training yourself not to worry is a choice which requires focus and application. Just dipping into this chapter on worrying and applying the strategies intermittently will most probably not be helpful. However, developing a toolkit of strategies which you can apply on a daily basis will increase your chances of successfully reducing worrying.

Example

Marisa was suffering with increased stress levels at work. A central component of her stress was worrying and she was increasingly worried about how her team and managers perceived her. More specifically she was worried that they didn't like her and as a consequence she found herself developing a 'chameleon-like personality'. In other words she was aiming to be liked by everyone, even the colleagues she had little in common with and would not usually chat with. In addition, when talking with colleagues she was worrying about saying the right thing. She found this process really stressful and tiring.

Initially Marisa addressed her views about worrying as she did believe that worrying about being liked helped to keep her on her toes and manage her professional relationships in a better way. After she recognized that this idea was really not beneficial she went on to make a list of the advantages and disadvantages of worrying in this situation. Once Marisa recognized the negative emotional and behavioural consequences of worrying, she made a list of reasons why not to worry. After reading that list on a daily basis over a period of one month, she found that she was able to bring her worrying under control and that her relationships with her colleagues was not the issue here, rather her worrying (which was triggered by an innocuous comment by a colleague) led her to over-focus on her relationships and look for evidence of difficulties in those relationships which weren't actually there.

The key learning point is that worrying, with time and effort, is amenable to change.

Chapter Seven
Managing stress

There is no doubt that workplace stress exists; the fact is that the experience of stress is now widespread and that a build up of it can lead to further (dis)stress and psychological ill health. The effects of stress impact on the individual not only in the short term but also in the long term, leading to psychological and physical problems for the individual that a ripple effect, impacting on relationships with colleagues, close friends and family.

According to the Health and Safety Executive (HSE, 2011) in 2010–11, 10.8 million days were lost as a result of work-related stress and depression and on average every case of stress, depression and anxiety led to 27.6 days away from work. More recently the cumulative effect of the economic recession has led to an exacerbation of symptoms of stress and mental health issues alike.

Stress is different to pressure: a certain amount of pressure is ubiquitous to all workplaces, and can be motivating, but pressure turns to stress when it becomes unrelenting. Here we aim to provide an overview of what stress means to the individual, as well as discussing the sources and symptoms of stress, before addressing the strategies to manage stress adequately.

What is stress?

There are many definitions of stress, for example the Health and Safety Executive have defined stress as 'The adverse reaction people have to excessive pressures or other types of demand placed on them' (2011), while Palmer *et al* assert that 'Stress occurs when the perceived pressure exceeds your ability to cope' (2003, p 2).

However you define stress, it is important to remember that stress is due to the internal psychological pressures experienced, often combined with the external organizational pressures/changes that are largely not within the individual's control.

Sources of work-related stress

According to the model of stress outlined below there are six major contributors to work-related stress. They are as follows:

1 The demands placed on employees, such as the working environment, and the volume and the complexity of the work, including the need to meet unrealistic deadlines.

2 The issue of control, that is how much say or how much involvement employees have in relation to their workload, whether they have too little or too much supervision or how much autonomy they have over their job.

3 How much support they receive, for example training received to do the job well, availability of resources, how much emphasis is placed on individual differences, and how much support is available from managers and peers.

4 Work relationships – how the organization promotes positive working relationships, how it addresses bullying, conflicts or harassment.

5 How well roles are defined. Are conflicting roles avoided or are roles clearly understood by employees?

6 Finally change – how well change is communicated to employees, eg the possibility of redundancy or being involved in a disciplinary process. Another source of occupational stress is restructuring which can undermine job security.

These six factors are embedded within the culture of the organization and relate to how the organization manages stress. Does it

FIGURE 7.1 Model of work stress

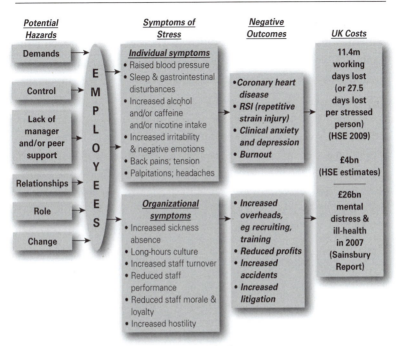

@ Adapted Palmer, Cooper & Thomas, 2001. Revised 2011

recognize it? What is the organization's stance on long hours? Are there adequate procedures in place to reduce stress? Are there support systems in place to help individuals eliminate stress?

The combination of culture and these factors lead to symptoms of stress and potential negative outcomes for both the individual and organization (see Figure 7.1).

Non-work-related factors that contribute to stress

In addition to the work-related contributions described above, Oliver and Lewis (2003) suggested that factors outside the work environment can also serve to heighten stress levels; these can include relationships, specifically the break-up of relationships, concerns about health, house moves, bereavement and managing specific difficulties relating to children.

Specific personality traits and attitudes can also impact on the individual's ability to cope with stress. For example, research conducted in the 1970s by Rosenman and his colleagues, who were cardiologists, highlighted the existence of two personality traits, Type A and Type B. They found that individuals who exhibited Type A behaviours were more likely to be impatient, competitive, fast eaters, quick walkers, with few interests outside work. These are the individuals who are at a higher risk of developing coronary heart disease, unlike the individuals who are Type B's, who are more easy-going and less competitive. Another concept, outlined by Rotter in the 1960s, is that of locus of control. He suggested that individuals who perceive that they are in control of their lives have an internal locus of control, while those who perceive that they have little control over what happens to them and may even see themselves as unlucky have an external locus of control.

One way of understanding locus of control is in terms of a continuum with the external and internal loci at opposite ends of the spectrum. The majority of people tend to land around the middle of the continuum; they know that they are generally in control of their lives and aim not to get stressed out about issues that are beyond their control. However, problems can occur if the individual experiences a series of events which in the main are outside their control, eg an increase in volume of work, illness of a partner or problems with the home, which combined with a negative attitude such as 'bad things always happen to me, I can't cope any more' can exacerbate the situation and lead to an increase in stress and decline in ability to cope.

As stated above, negative attitudes referred to in previous chapters also play a part in the development and maintenance of stress. Generally, core beliefs which centre on a lack of belief in one's own abilities, eg 'I'm not good enough', or the need to be 'perfect', together with negative beliefs, eg 'I must aim to meet all my deadlines regardless of the cost' and 'I'm rubbish at my job', can serve to exacerbate stress reactions.

How stress develops

The development model of stress outlined in Figure 7.2 highlights how an individual can develop symptoms of stress. An example of how Susan begun to feel stressed follows.

FIGURE 7.2   Model of stress

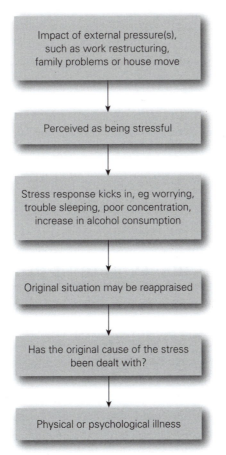

(Adapted from Palmer and Strickland, 1996)

Susan's department was subject to redundancies; three people left the team and their work was assimilated by those who were left. Susan took on a number of new tasks, which she found difficult to understand as there was no handover from the colleagues who were made redundant. To try and cope with her new role Susan began to work longer hours. As a result her work–life balance begun to suffer and she began to feel 'overwhelmed'. She started to worry about her work and her forthcoming appraisal in three months' time. She was concerned that unless she was able to show her manager that, as always, she was 'on top' of her work her appraisal would be negative. She struggled to fall asleep as her concerns about work went 'round and round' in her mind. She noticed feeling tense and began to experience tension headaches, and despite talking to her manager about how she could develop her role, her situation at work did not change. She stated that for the moment her only option was 'to knuckle down and get on with it'; this meant a continuation of long hours. Her tendency to feel overwhelmed increased until after two months she began to experience panic attacks and finally saw her GP to talk about her situation.

The effects and symptoms of stress

From a physiological perspective stress is a normal response to danger or threat. Known as 'automatic arousal' this response leads to 'fight or flight', and while this was useful for our ancestors, experiencing this response in the office or home on a regular basis can lead to symptoms of stress. In essence the hypothalamus part of the brain controls your reaction to stress; it impacts on the autonomic nervous system (ANS), which is composed of two parts; the sympathetic nervous system (SNS) and the parasympathetic nervous system (PNS). The SNS prepares your body for flight or flights, while the PNS aids relaxation. In stressful situations the arousal of the SNS leads to an increase in heart rate, perspiration, muscle tension and mental activity. If the person perceives that the stressful situation has ended, then the PNS helps the body to relax or

TABLE 7.1 Symptoms of stress

Behavioural symptoms	Physical symptoms	Psychological symptoms
Irritability	Nausea	Feeling miserable, anxious, angry, depressed, guilty, ashamed, hurt or suicidal
Aggression	Headaches	
Increase in alcohol consumption	Rapid heartbeat	
Restlessness	Dizziness/feeling faint	Feeling out of control or helpless
Teeth grinding	Tightness in the chest	Trouble concentrating
Comfort eating	Excessive sweating	Daydreaming
Poor sleep	Butterflies in your stomach	Negative/unhelpful thinking such as 'This is awful', 'I can't cope', 'Everyone thinks I'm useless', 'I'm going mad', 'I'll never feel better'
Withdrawal or sulking	Pain	
Lack of interest in sex	Indigestion	
Eating/walking faster	Diarrhoea	
Poor driving	Constipation	
Poor time management	Allergies/skin rashes	
Poor eye contact	Lowered immune system	Lack of self-confidence
Withdrawal from work and in personal relationships		Low self-esteem
Increase in caffeine use		
Compulsive or impulsive behaviour		
Impaired speech or voice tremor		
Avoidance behaviour		

reach a stage of equilibrium. However, the frequent and prolonged action of this system can lead to stress. The main symptoms of stress are listed in Table 7.1.

Strategies to manage stress

Most of the strategies discussed in this book can be applied to stress management. In addition there are techniques included in this section which are mainly applicable to the management of pressure. Finding and then applying the right blend of strategies is the most effective way of dealing with stress, in combination with the development of a stress management action plan.

Restructuring your negative perceptions

In Chapter 2 we discussed the impact and restructuring of negative perceptions, as this type of thinking can play a part in the development and maintenance of pressure. Table 7.2 – in this case filled out by Patricia – highlights how stress-evoking perceptions can be reconstructed using an automatic form.

Working through your core beliefs

Often during intense periods of stress, core beliefs are activated, and these thoughts are often rigid and restrictive. To see if your core beliefs impact on your ability to manage stress levels aim to use the process outlined in Figure 7.3, which Patricia used to isolate her core belief.

Take an issue that is causing you stress and ask yourself 'Let's suppose that is true, what does that mean to me?' Then question every answer you give by asking, 'What does that mean to me? This form of questioning should help you identify your own core belief. Do bear in mind that it is not always necessary to work with both core beliefs and negative perceptions; restructuring the latter can also be sufficient in bring about a change in mood and behaviour and an improvement in stress levels.

To address her core belief, Patricia used a cost-benefit analysis form (see Table 7.3) to look at the pros and cons of holding onto this belief. The cons of holding onto this belief far outweighed the pros. On this basis Patricia then went on to consider how she would like to see herself. Her more compassionate replacement core belief was, 'I'm OK, I don't need to do EVERYTHING perfectly.'

TABLE 7.2 Reconstructing stress-evoking perceptions

Stress Inducing Situation (SIS)	Stress Evoking Perceptions (SEP)	Emotion and physical symptoms	Restructuring	Stress Reducing Perceptions (SRP)	Impact
Conference call with European counterparts and managers to discuss delineation of work	This call is going to be bad As usual, I'll be landed with all the difficult jobs My manager won't support me if I speak out about the delineation I'll end up working an 11 hour day to get everything finished	Feeling stressed Headache Tense neck Sweaty palms	Try not to jump to conclusions Stop predicting negative outcomes Remember you have done this before (lots of times), got worked up and the outcome was OK Prepare for it beforehand, be proactive, speak to Martyn (manager)	I don't know this for certain Don't catastrophize, decide what jobs I'll be willing to do beforehand and keep to this Speak to Martyn tomorrow and ask him to support me during the meeting This won't happen if I keep to the plan	Reduction in stress due to change in thinking about the conference call and development of plan.

TABLE 7.3   Patricia's cost–benefit analysis form

I'm a waste of space

Benefits	Costs
Keeps me focused	It may keep me focused but I get stressed every time I have a project to complete, which is not good for me
This is my driver, if I let go of this I won't push myself so hard	This driver is making me ill and tense
It helps me feel more in control	Being in control does not involve having migraines, insomnia and feeling panicky
Other people like and respect me because I have high standards	Even if I lower my standards a bit other people will still like me and respect me. I know plenty of people at work who are doing well and don't have such high standards Thinking I'm a waste of space makes me feel miserable I've actually achieved a lot in my life which I conveniently forget about

New core belief:
I'm OK, I don't need to do EVERYTHING perfectly.

Working with your perfectionist tendencies

Pushing yourself or wanting to do things 'right', aiming to keep standards high, is not an unusual trait. Most people would argue that aiming high is motivational and that it enhances both personal and professional performance. However, there is a big difference between relentlessly pushing yourself no matter what in order to achieve, setting your standards so high that you can't reach them, and working hard to do extremely well.

FIGURE 7.3   Core belief identification

Identify a situation you want to work on

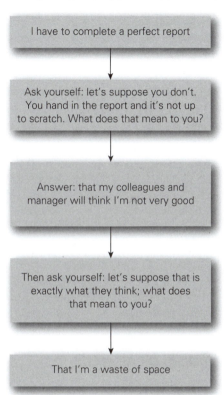

Here are some common perfectionist beliefs:

- No one can do it as well as I can.
- It can always be better.
- Excellence limits chaos.
- I need to stay in control all the time.
- If you can't do it right it's not worth doing at all.

- Everything in my life needs to be perfect.
- Other people need to meet my expectations.
- Being the best is all important.
- If I don't do my best I've failed.

Research into perfectionism has highlighted the negative impact on health that striving towards impossibly high standards leads to, such as: stress, depression, anxiety, worrying, low self-worth, obsessive–compulsive disorders and even eating disorders. Psychological functioning can also be impaired. Individuals with perfectionist tendencies tend be very critical of themselves; they compare themselves to others who they perceive have done better whether in professional or personal spheres, or even both; they judge themselves as failures or as 'not good enough' if they fail to achieve their goals because their self-esteem is linked to their performance; and they often put off doing tasks because they are concerned they will not perform the task to the standards they have set themselves. Perfectionists often tend to over-check their work, they can be prolific list makers and they can have difficulty making decisions in order to avoid making the wrong ones.

Can perfectionism be altered?

The answer to that is 'yes', but in order for that to happen it requires a readiness to change and insight into your own perfectionist drives. The process of change needs sustained effort, planning and a methodological application of strategies within the context of a predetermined concrete time frame.

It's important to remember that everyone is different in their attitude towards and management of perfectionism. Some people refuse to relinquish their perfectionist drives despite recognizing the costs to them, others want to make changes only to certain aspects of their perfectionism, while yet others choose to work on all their perfectionist tendencies.

The change strategies

When working with the thoughts and behaviours that drive perfectionism, the first step in this process of change is to look at the costs and benefits or the pros and cons of changing your attitude(s). Do this in writing, not in your head. Use time projection to consider the impact on work performance if you don't make the changes and then again if you do make them. Most people recognize that unless they make some adjustments they will continue to put themselves under unrelenting pressure which may over time lead to an increase in psychological and physical problems.

Challenging your perfectionist attitudes

Aim to identify the situations in which your perfectionist beliefs are strong and then apply the questions below together with the Socratic questions outlined in Chapter 2 to dispute your thinking and to replace your inflexible beliefs with more flexible ones.

Questions to ask of your perfectionist beliefs

- Is there another way of looking at this situation?

- What would a friend or colleague say in this situation?

- Am I asking too much of myself?

- How does this line of thinking impact on myself and others?

- Just because I believe I should do things exactly right does that mean everything should always go exactly to plan?

- Can I learn to consider the middle ground here instead of always jumping to extremes?

- What exactly is the middle ground here?

- Can I really be in control 100 per cent of the time?

- Just because I don't do something to the best of my ability does that make me a failure/worthless/or a fraud?

The flawed link between actions and self-esteem

We have observed that individuals often connect their actions to their self-esteem. For example, Daniel believed that when his manager questioned the viability of the statistics he used in a team presentation, his manager thought that his whole presentation was rubbish. As he always aimed for perfection, he jumped to the conclusion that he was a failure for delivering a substandard presentation. He then went on to to worry about his overall performance within the company; he even imagined being reprimanded by the partners and then being given a verbal warning. In this case Daniel jumped to the conclusion that not doing a task exactly right made him a failure as solicitor.

Individuals who make the link between their behaviours and self-esteem run the risk of feeling bad when the outcome of their actions do not go exactly to plan. To counter this way of thinking, the therapist worked with Daniel to help him see that doing a task imperfectly did not and would never make him a failure.

An excerpt from the therapy follows:

Therapist: So Daniel, using alternative statistics in the presentation to those that your manager thought were appropriate makes you a failure?

Daniel: Yes, I'm failing in my job.

Therapist: How do you feel now, as you are talking about this?

Daniel: Terrible. I feel really depressed.

Therapist: So based on our previous discussion can you see that this is all or nothing thinking and that if you continue to go down this route you will most probably make yourself depressed every time something at work doesn't go exactly to plan? Do you want to keep doing this for the rest of your career?

Daniel: I can see it's counterproductive, but it's just what I'm used to doing and I don't know how to change it.

Therapist: OK, to start with are you telling me that you really are a complete failure at work?

Daniel: Well no.

Therapist: OK, so let's look at the last month, tell me what has gone
             well at work, we'll make a list together.

(To help Daniel recognize that he was discounting the positive things
that happened at work, he and the therapist made a list of all the
things that had gone well.)

Therapist: Now let me ask you would you also call your wife
             a failure is she makes a mistake at work?

Daniel: No, but I know that I have a tendency to be harder on
             myself than others.

Therapist: OK, would you recommend this strategy to others?

Daniel: No.

Therapist: Well that's double standards; you need to treat yourself
             as you would other people.

Daniel: I know I need to keep working on that.

Therapist: OK, in addition you need to stop labelling yourself here.
             There is no such person as a 'total failure'. Using different
             statistics to what your boss expected you to use doesn't
             make you a failure, only a human being who made a
             choice that your boss didn't like. So to sum up, try to
             catch yourself when you start to go down this spiral, use
             the strategies we have discussed to stop yourself feeling
             down. Don't forget to remind yourself on a regular basis
             of what you have achieved.

If you recognize that your own self-esteem is linked to your
performance, aim to break this connection; work on disputing
your perfectionist thoughts. Ask yourself does labelling yourself
as a failure, useless or not good enough, hinder or facilitate your
performance? Remember that one mistake or missed deadline
does not make you a failure/useless or not good enough; to be a
total failure you would need to perform really badly at everything
you do.

The better choice is self-acceptance rather than self-esteem

One of the problems with self-esteem as we have seen above is that it can fluctuate according to how we feel from one day to the next. It can depend on numerous factors which leads to a yo-yo effect. If somebody says something positive about you or your work you feel good, but on the other hand if somebody says something you perceive as negative, you feel bad. Because of this, in recent years psychologists and therapists have focused more on self-acceptance rather than self-esteem. Individuals are incredibly complex beings; in fact we are a mix of traits, features and actions, some of which we accept as fact (eg I have brown hair), some of which we can work on (eg my driving skills or my presentation skills) and that not one of these traits or actions represents us in our totality or as a whole. On this basis they state that it's important not to rate ourselves as a whole, for example completely rubbish or useless. Rather we should rate our behaviours or only certain aspects of ourselves: for example it is better to think 'I messed up my interview this time, I'll work harder on the preparation next time', as opposed to 'I'm so stupid for having not got that job.'

The Big I and little i is a helpful way of illustrating the concept of self-acceptance. Going back to the example of Daniel, in addition to helping him recognize the futility of labelling himself, the therapist introduced him to the Big I and little i. He drew a Big I filled with lots of small i's which represented all Daniel's features, values and behaviours. The therapist then pointed to one of the small i's and wrote next to it 'used alternative statistics in the presentation'. He then reminded Daniel that this one action did not represent him as whole, that it didn't define him because he is much more complicated than that. To reinforce this, the therapist asked Daniel to think about what other features made him who he is today, and what Daniel noted is shown in Figure 7.4. Daniel was then able to recognize that rating himself on the basis of one i was not OK; rather he needed to accept himself as he was, a person who was not defined by the one action or feature.

FIGURE 7.4   Daniel's completed Big I and Little i form

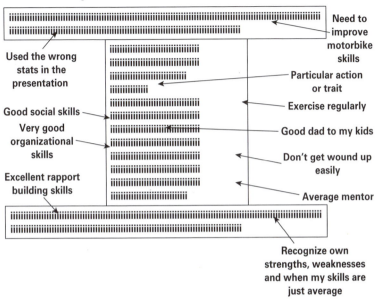

Daniel's Big I & Little i

Need to improve motorbike skills

Used the wrong stats in the presentation

Particular action or trait

Good social skills

Exercise regularly

Very good organizational skills

Good dad to my kids

Excellent rapport building skills

Don't get wound up easily

Average mentor

Recognize own strengths, weaknesses and when my skills are just average

The continuum method

This method is very helpful for those individuals who think in extremes and as a consequence tend to ignore the middle ground. The continuum outlined below illustrates how Jamie managed his extreme thinking and illustrates the process for working on your own extreme thinking. An extended continuum form is available in Appendix G.

Jamie's continuum

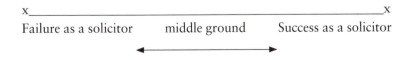

x——————————————————————————————x
Failure as a solicitor   middle ground   Success as a solicitor

Jamie believed that to be a successful solicitor you always had to strive for perfection and for the ultimate goal, partnership; not doing so made you a failure. In this instance Jamie focused on what the middle ground was, after discussion with his friend and conducting a mini-survey which he did to find out if his friends who worked as solicitors for other firms had ever aimed for less than perfection. (Two had – one was doing well, the other had to take time out from work due to burnout – and three were considering if they could face the pressure of going for partnership.) Jamie established the middle ground:

'If I relentlessly push for success all the time I will make myself ill,
I have to accept myself as I am – a good motivated solicitor who works hard and cannot always give or achieve 100 per cent. If I make partner that is great but I am not going to kill myself doing it.'

Managing self-criticism

Often a crucial element of perfectionism is protracted self-criticism, a tendency to label yourself negatively for having made any mistakes. If you recognize this process, ask yourself: does berating yourself make you feel better or worse? How does it help you in the short and long term to do your work well? Is this a strategy you would recommend to others? If not why not?

Hopefully asking yourself these questions will highlight the ineffectiveness of this process; instead compile a list stating why self-criticism is not helpful. Keep this list with you and read it every day, adding new reasons if you want.

Example

Maria recognized that her perfectionism in her workplace was causing her stress and that her behavior of repeatedly checking her work was time-consuming, but she didn't know how to start making changes. She was also worried that 'doing things differently' would impact negatively on her performance. Her vicious cycle of thinking and actions is outlined in Figure 7.5.

FIGURE 7.5 Maria's vicious cycle of thinking

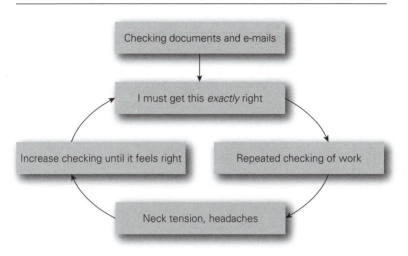

Maria made the choice to focus only on her work-related perfectionism as at home both she and her husband shared the desire to keep the house spotless, very tidy and ordered; they worked well as a team and shared the same goals.

To start with Maria made a list of the pros and cons of completing all her work to her high standards: her cost–benefit analysis is shown in Table 7.4.

Before completing the chart Maria was convinced that her attitude had many benefits, and it was only after completing the cost–benefit analysis that she was able to see that the benefits were practically non-existent. Her one belief that completing her work to high standards was motivating was challenged by her therapist. In addition, to reinforce her motivation to change, she and her therapist used time projection, focusing on the next two years. Maria focused on how her performance at work would develop, taking into account the costs to herself if she didn't address her high standards and how performance would develop if she did make the necessary changes.

The third step towards change involved finding an alternative belief to 'all my work needs to be completed to my high standards', based on the impact her belief had on her performance. Maria stated that she would prefer to think, 'I want to do really well at work, but if I don't always, I'm not going to give myself a hard

TABLE 7.4   Maria's cost–benefit analysis form

All my work needs to be completed to my high standards

Costs	Benefits
Constantly stressed	It makes me motivated to try harder
Stay late to check everything is done right	
Worry and more worry about work while at home	
Put off new tasks because they are overwhelming	
Feel stuck and indecisive	
Put myself down even when I receive good feedback	
Disappointment	

time.' Maria and her therapist then explored the impact her alternative thinking would have on her mood; she acknowledged that this type of thinking would leave her feeling less stressed and tense.

Lastly Maria addressed the behaviours that needed to change to reduce the pressure on her; she agreed that once she had written her e-mails she would only check them once before sending. She also agreed to check her reports once and then provide feedback to her therapist on the consequences of these changes. She predicted that her boss and colleagues would find errors in her work and bring them to her attention, leaving her feeling distressed. In fact nothing happened. She did miss out some full stops and apostrophes in her work; however nobody noticed, which reminded her that her standards were higher than those of others. At the same time Maria and her therapist also addressed her self-criticism which also maintained her high standards, as when Maria believed that she had not achieved she criticized herself. She called herself 'stupid' and an 'idiot' to motivate herself to do better, but the effect was to make her feel worse and it inhibited her performance. To reinforce this Maria made the following list, which she headed 'The reasons why I don't need to criticize myself':

- Self-criticism makes me feel miserable.
- Self-criticism leads to negative thinking.
- Self-criticism makes me feel stuck.
- Self-criticism is an ineffectual use of time.

Pulling it all together

Having recognized your own stress triggers, the next logical step is to develop your own action plan and then to act on it. Remember 'don't stew', use all the relevant strategies outlined in this book to make a comprehensive personalized plan to address all the aspects of stress. An example of a completed stress management plan is outlined in Figure 7.6.

FIGURE 7.6   A completed stress management plan

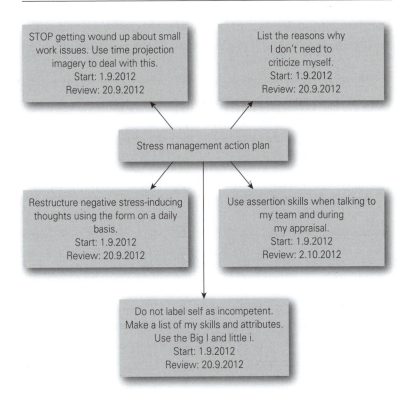

Chapter Eight
How to manage your angry feelings

A nger is an intrinsic human emotion; it's a normal human reaction which can be a catalyst for change; and it can promote dialogue and problem solving. However, frequent incidents of anger which seem to spiral out of control in inappropriate environments such as the office or the car can be a signal that your anger needs to be managed in a more productive way. In order to understand and manage anger better, in this chapter we focus on the causes and symptoms of anger, before addressing the strategies you can employ to keep anger at bay.

Why do individuals feel angry?

The reasons for anger vary tremendously and can include events outside our personal control, such as strikes, redundancies, team members not pulling their weight and traffic jams. Our own actions can also trigger anger, for example not completing a task very well or losing a work tender. Other triggers can be due to a perceived infringement of our own moral codes, values or views which we hold strongly or even excessive deliberation on a specific issue. For example, Michael felt very angry when he was overlooked for promotion; the promotion was given instead to a colleague who was younger than him and had been with the company for less time. Michael believed that he had been treated unfairly. The more he thought about the situation the angrier he felt. Even seeing his colleague in the office induced tension and Michael found it difficult to concentrate on his work. In another example, Adrianna expressed anger when another team member was not disciplined for coming in late on a regular basis, while when she came in late one day her manager expressed annoyance with her unpunctuality.

Other contributing factors for feeling angry include ongoing stress levels, depression and tiredness. In addition childhood experiences can also play a part in our ability to express and manage anger. Megan, a senior consultant, was taught as a child that anger was not an acceptable emotion to express. As a result she tended to internalize her anger. In her role she was under pressure to perform and as this pressure increased she began to feel more and more angry. Instead of voicing her concerns she complained bitterly to her colleagues about the partner in the firm who was directing the project. Megan stopped working so hard and left work early to show her displeasure about the project. Ultimately her passive-aggressive manner only served to maintain her anger and led to problems within the team and with the partner involved.

When considering your own feelings of anger, it's important to try to consider the combination of factors that may lead to your outbursts.

When anger becomes a problem

The acronym FIND (see Figure 8.1) is a good reminder to act on your feelings of anger. Over a longer period of time, periods of anger can build up, leading to an increase in intensity and aggression or even moments of rage. So, remember: 'when you FIND then act'.

Symptoms of anger

Figure 8.2 underlines some of the main symptoms of anger, while Figure 8.3 highlights a cycle of anger outlined by client Paul who came for therapy to address his anger. Paul had worked in banking for 12 years. As he was promoted up the ladder his responsibilities increased and over the past 18 months he was under pressure to

FIGURE 8.1   Using FIND to act on your feelings of anger

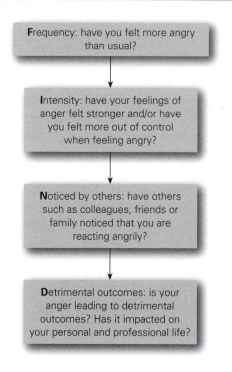

Frequency: have you felt more angry than usual?

Intensity: have your feelings of anger felt stronger and/or have you felt more out of control when feeling angry?

Noticed by others: have others such as colleagues, friends or family noticed that you are reacting angrily?

Detrimental outcomes: is your anger leading to detrimental outcomes? Has it impacted on your personal and professional life?

complete a growing number of projects, leading to long hours, more stress and a poor work–life balance. The trigger for his anger was the cancellation of a holiday he had booked with his family. He was asked to cancel his holiday by his manager as the project he was coordinating had run over its deadline. Paul was very angry about the cancellation and found that his feelings of anger were interfering with his ability to complete the project.

Managing anger

In this section we outline the strategies that can be adopted to identify and manage anger. It is important to remember that when your anger is reaching its peak or is at its peak, controlling your mood is

FIGURE 8.2   Some symptoms of anger

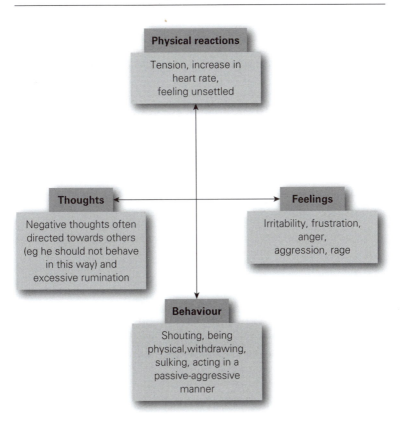

hard to do; therefore it's beneficial to try and manage anger away before it reaches its pinnacle.

Determine the triggers for your anger

After having used FIND to identify if you have an anger problem, aim to isolate the probable trigger(s) for your anger and then your specific reaction(s), which will most certainly be comprised of a combination of actions, physiological responses and negative thoughts related to the trigger event(s). One of the easiest ways to do this is to keep a note of your experiences over a period of 3–4 weeks using the worksheet in Appendix H.

FIGURE 8.3   Results of feelings of anger

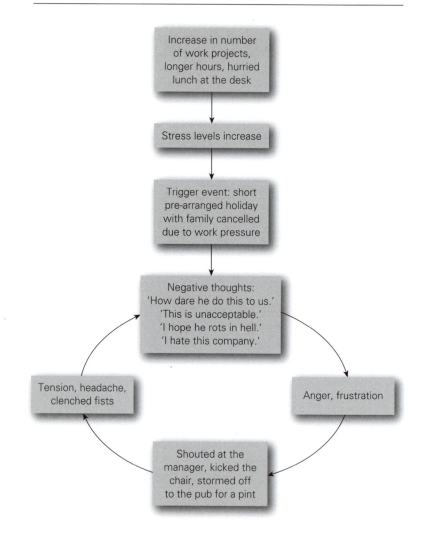

Link anger-inducing triggers to your reactions using the worksheet

Having identified your triggers and reactions, think of the process in terms of an upward spiral (see Figure 8.4). Once you react in anger to a trigger, it is easy for your feelings and thoughts to spiral

FIGURE 8.4   The upward anger spiral

Anger at its worst

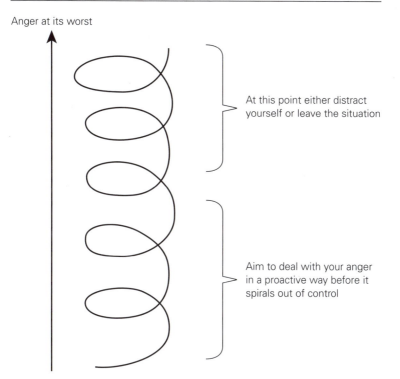

At this point either distract yourself or leave the situation

Aim to deal with your anger in a proactive way before it spirals out of control

quickly until you may feel out of control. Once that happens it is very difficult to stop and manage your anger. The solution is to catch your anger before it hits the halfway spiral mark, then you have a better chance of controlling it. The key to this is recognition of the process and practice to stop it.

While avoiding triggers for anger as a short-term strategy can work, in the long term avoidance can bring with it additional complications.

Other strategies

There are several other strategies to catch your anger and stop it spiralling out of control.

> ### Example
>
> Simon recognized that his colleague Colin was gossiping about his private life and the content of the gossip was untrue and quite trite. Simon did not want to confront Colin as he 'didn't like confrontations' and said that Colin was an extremely difficult person to talk to. For Simon, avoiding Colin as much as he could worked for three months, but when his daughter came home from school to say that her classmates were gossiping about her, Simon found he was so angry he nearly broke a chair at home. He recognized that his over-reaction was down to the fact that the gossiping at work was ongoing and that while he strongly believed that 'gossiping was a poisonous process that should not be tolerated' he was the one that was not doing anything to stop it. Therefore he was acting against his own strongly held values. So for him pretending the problem did not exist just wasn't sustainable.

Disputing anger-inducing thoughts

In Chapter 2 we outlined some of the most common thinking errors. Some of these categories of thinking relate to anger more than others, and include:

Low frustration tolerance:	'I can't stand this'
Catastrophizing:	'This is the worst thing that has ever happened'
Demands:	'He should not be such an idiot'
Magnification:	'I'll never get over this'
Mind reading:	'He did that on purpose to undermine me'
Labelling:	'I'm incompetent'
Personalization:	'That look was directed at me'
All or nothing thinking:	'The lack of a pay rise means my career is finished'

As stated in the other chapters of this book, the way we feel is down to the way we think, as Rian McMullin (2000), a psychologist in the United States, suggested emotions can motivate people to act but they don't make them respond. Therefore working with negative thinking styles or errors and questioning them is a necessary step in disarming anger. To do this you can use the automatic negative thought form available in Appendix A.

The following questions and statements are particularly effective in disarming anger:

- What makes you say that you can't stand the situation?
- Have you stood more difficult situations in the past?
- What did you do?
- Have bad things happened before?
- How did you cope?
- How would other people you know cope?
- Are you demanding that other people change?
- Where does that get you (other than wound up)?
- Modify your demands; make them into preferences.
- Stop imagining the worse, it makes you feel bad.
- When was the last time your mind-reading skills worked for you?
- Remind yourself to stop mind reading. If indeed you were so good at it you would not be working where you are now, rather you would be earning a lot of money and appearing on stage or TV.
- If you are taking comments or actions personally, think of the other possible reasons for the comments or actions.
- Would you recommend that other colleagues and friends also take the same comments personally?
- Stop labelling yourself or others; it's counterproductive and only maintains your anger.
- Is there a rule in the world that states that everything should go exactly the way you want it to go?
- Think 'middle ground', don't think in extremes.

Here are some realistic responses to the negative thoughts outlined earlier:

- 'I can't stand this' – 'I can stand it even if I don't like it'.
- 'This is the worst thing that has ever happened' – 'I can cope with this, I have to'.
- 'He should not be such an idiot' – I can't change other people, it's impossible; but I can change how I respond and not get so wound up about it'.
- 'I'll never get over this' – 'This is jumping way ahead and making me feel worse; I can deal with it step by step'.
- 'He did that on purpose to undermine me' – 'I don't know that this is strictly true; can there be another explanation?'
- 'I'm incompetent' – 'I mustn't wind myself up. It's not true, if it was I wouldn't be here today'.
- 'That look was directed at me' – 'I don't know that for sure'.
- 'The lack of a pay rise means my career is finished – 'I'm not the only one who did not get a pay rise'.

If possible distance yourself physically from the source of your anger: leave the situation and go and do something different, break the cycle. If in applying the upward anger spiral you recognize your anger starting to escalate to the point of no return, try to leave the room. If possible verbalize your intention: for example say, 'I'm feeling annoyed, and before I say something I regret, I'm leaving the room and will come back to talk about this when I have calmed down.'

Breathing

Use breathing techniques to calm your physiological response to anger. Aim to breathe from your abdomen, not your chest (this can make your anger worse). Breathe in through you nose slowly and then breathe out slowly. Focus on this process; continue to do it until you feel less angry. This can be done discreetly and is best practised outside the situation in the first instance.

Practise relaxation techniques

If you practise relaxation techniques on a regular basis (ie every day or every other day), you will find it easier to stop the physiological spiral of anger and be able to think more clearly. The relaxation techniques outlined in Chapter 4 are an excellent starting point.

Another strategy is to repeat a calming word to yourself such as 'calm', 'relax' or 'soothe', or another word which you find relaxing.

Jerry Deffenbacher (1996) suggests visualizing yourself as a turtle with a tough shell, so all the unwanted comments just bounce of the shell; or as duck, so that negative comments wash off your tightly-knit, waterproof feathers straight into the water.

Reflect on your past reactions

If you find that you react angrily in the same type of situations or even with the same person, reflect on how you can act differently, and write down your new reactions.

Example

Martha found herself feeling frustrated and angry when speaking to her New York work counterpart Claire on the telephone or when seeing her face to face once a month. She recognized that a certain proportion of Claire's comments and actions ignited the situation, so she made a list of 'different things to do and say when in conversation and meetings with Claire'. This helped her to manage their interactions in a better way.

Exercise

Exercise can be used as an adjunct to manage anger; it's a good outlet but on its own it will most probably not reduce anger.

Other strategies

Other strategies include being assertive and standing up for yourself without being aggressive. Information about assertion strategies is outlined in Chapter 12. Problem-solving your anger is also advantageous and effectual. Making a decision and action planning changes following an anger-inducing event is practical and resilience enhancing. For example, Michael, who was mentioned earlier, after some weeks recognized the negative impact of his dwelling on his lack of promotion and instead chose to do something about it. He spoke to his manager about the situation, outlining his views, and asked for clarification on this matter. He channelled his anger in a proactive manner. An blank problem-solving form, 'PRACTICE', is available in Appendix E for you to use in this context.

Chapter Nine
Managing responses to trauma

In recent years, with the increase in focus on UK and worldwide terrorist activities, the issue of how to deal with traumatic incidents has received greater attention both in professional and public domains. Bearing this in mind, in this chapter we address traumatic experiences, what they constitute, the main symptoms of trauma and how to manage it.

What constitutes a trauma?

The term 'trauma' comes from an ancient word which means to wound. A traumatic incident can involve a car or train accident, an assault, such as a robbery, which can include a sexual component such as rape, or a terrorist attack or a natural disaster such as a flood or storm.

Initial and long-term reactions to trauma vary from person to person, and it is also important to remember that just witnessing or watching a traumatic incident, let's say on television, can lead to symptoms of trauma: this is referred to as 'vicarious learning'.

The three key features of trauma

1 Re-experiencing the trauma: re-experiencing can take the form of distressing memories/thoughts/feelings/images about the trauma. For example, David, who was in a car accident, found

that when he was driving the image of the accident popped into his head. As a result he felt anxious and panicky and found it hard to concentrate on the road. The more he worried about the image, the more he experienced it whilst driving.

Another feature of re-experiencing can be dreams or nightmares, which can be linked to the incident or previous experiences, or seem to be unrelated to the current trauma. Some people also experience flashbacks which can occur without warning and involve a sense that the trauma is happening right now. Flashbacks can feel debilitating and overwhelming. Following an assault by a man smelling of aftershave, whenever Paula smelled strong perfumes she found herself feeling as if she was there again, at the time of the assault.

2 Attempting to avoid anything to do with the trauma: this can include avoiding going near the location of the trauma, blocking out thoughts of the trauma, people associated with it and actively pushing memories of the trauma out of your mind.

3 Increased sense of arousal: this results in problems with falling asleep or staying asleep; problems with your concentration; feeling angry or irritable; and a tendency towards excessive vigilance, which can involve 'being on the look out for danger'. For example, after his motorbike accident Anil started to worry about other drivers. He lectured his colleagues who came to work on motorbikes and attempted to check their bikes to make sure they were roadworthy. In Anil's mind all motorbikes now represented danger.

The final component of the increased sense of arousal is an exaggerated startle response which includes feeling more jumpy and more easily startled then you would have done before the trauma.

In addition to the features outlined above, some of the more common symptoms of trauma are listed in Table 9.1. Experiencing a trauma can also lead to other psychological problems, such as anxiety, depression and substance misuse, or it can exacerbate current problems you may be experiencing.

TABLE 9.1　Common reactions to trauma

Physical signs	Emotional signs
Feeling tired	Anxiety
Increase in aches and pains	Shame
Tension	Guilt
Nausea and stomach problems	Fear
Increase in your startle response	Depression
	Anger
	Blame
	Frustration
	Panic
	Irritability
	Denial
	Helplessness
	Shock
	Sadness

Behavioural signs	Cognitive signs
Tendency towards withdrawal	Flashbacks and excessive worrying and thinking about the trauma and your current experience and future.
Loss or increase in appetite	Examples of thoughts include:
Increase in alcohol consumption	Why did this happen to me?
Sleep problems	Why aren't I feeling better?
Tendency to be hyperactive	It's my fault
Increase in smoking	Nobody can understand how I feel
Loss of interest in usual everyday activities	The world really is an awful place
	I'm going mad
	It could happen again
	I'll never get better
	My life is over
	I can't cope with this

Overall the experience of trauma can have reverberations on so many aspects of daily life. From your working life, to your relationships and physical health, and it can also lead to financial problems. Following his motorbike accident Anil found that in addition to his jumpiness he felt really angry at times. This impacted on work and his relationship with his partner. Andy was unused to feeling angry and didn't know how to manage his reaction. He then started worrying when redundancies were announced at work because he felt that he would be the first to go because of his angry outbursts at work. In addition his relationship with his partner had changed as he found her 'light attitude to life' irritating and her humour annoying. He managed his irritation towards her by consuming more wine at home and this in turn led to an increase in arguments with his girlfriend. Consequently his stress levels increased and he began to feel angry and confused for feeling the way he was feeling, with no solution in sight.

The initial steps involved in recovering from a traumatic incident

Remember that experiencing some or all of the symptoms outlined in Table 9.1 is a normal reaction to an abnormal event. These symptoms may take some time to ease and you may even feel well after the trauma, but then the symptoms can 'hit you in the face' some time after the incident. There is no 'right' way to feel after a traumatic incident.

If you have just experienced a traumatic incident, it is important that you treat yourself with compassion and kindness, and try to follow the guidelines below:

- Remember that your reactions to the event are typical reactions that others have experienced to an atypical event.
- If you want to talk about the incident do so. Find a friend or family member who is a good listener and tell them about what happened and how you are feeling at the moment.

- Do not spend much time on your own; instead arrange to spend time with family or friends even if you don't engage in conversations with them.

- Do not attempt to make any major decisions during the month or so after the incident. There will be plenty of time to do this later.

- Be kind to yourself; make a list of things that you can do which make you happy and you enjoy, for example watching the sunset, going for walks, watching films, talking to friends and reading.

- Try not to use alcohol or drugs to help you cope, as this will make you feel worse and have an adverse effect on your ability to cope.

- Do not push yourself to do anything that you don't want to do.

If you are helping another person who has experienced a trauma consider the following guidelines:

- Remember that they are recovering from a trauma, so their reactions may be a little different to normal.

- Do not push the person to talk, but if they want to talk be ready to listen.

- If possible help the person maintain a near to normal routine.

- Recognize that recovery can take time, do not impose your own views on what they should be doing or thinking.

How to manage your recovery process from trauma

The process of recovery can take weeks or months; it varies from person to person and can depend on the kind of trauma you experienced, whether you have experienced a previous traumatic incident, how you were feeling prior to the trauma and what kind of support you receive afterwards.

It is preferable to cope with the trauma head on as opposed to trying not to think about it or pretend that is hasn't happened. This may seem counterintuitive and frightening but it is the best thing to do, as processing your traumatic experience leads to a reduction in symptoms, while ignoring what happened just keeps the trauma experience alive in your mind. In the late 1990s Richards and Lovell suggested that you see your mind as a processing plant or factory which stores all your experiences. These all come into your mind via a conveyor belt. Everyday experiences just sit on the conveyor belt and are processed and stored neatly in your mind. However, because traumatic experiences are out of the ordinary and cannot be processed so easily, they stop the conveyor belt from moving forward. These experiences need to be processed before they are put back on the conveyor belt and finally stored. To do this it is important to be proactive in dealing with your response(s) to trauma and to develop a series of constructive coping strategies to address your reaction(s). Below is a list of techniques you can use to aid the recovery process.

Constructive coping strategies

Talk or write about the trauma: if you choose to talk about it do so with a trusted friend; talk about what happened, how you felt, what you thought and how you feel now. Attempt not to edit your narrative and be honest in your conversation.

If you decide to write about the trauma you have a number of options: you can write about your experiences prior to the trauma with a particular emphasis on your positive 'feel good' experiences, then about the trauma and finally about how you see your future; or you can write only about the trauma in as much detail as possible. This can be quite anxiety provoking and may take a few goes, which is fine. To process the memory of the trauma try to reread what you have written on a daily basis until you feel OK and not tense or anxious reading your narrative or story. If more information about what happened comes to mind include it in the written narrative and keep reading. Initially you may feel uncomfortable doing this and this is a normal reaction. Bear in mind that the more

Example

After being involved in a car accident, Pam was anxious about driving again; even thinking about driving made her heart race and she felt dizzy and fearful. Pam wanted to get behind the wheel again, so together with her therapist she developed a plan to address her fear using a procedure called graded exposure. (Another example of how to implement this technique is highlighted in Chapter 5.) She discussed the situations connected with driving which caused her anxiety, rated how anxiety-provoking each situation was on a scale of 0–10, with 10 representing the highest level of anxiety and 0 the lowest, and then made a list of the situations to tackle, starting with the easiest one first. She agreed to address each event in order, so initially she chose just to stand next to the car with her hand on the bonnet. She rated her anxiety as 4 as she was engaged in this task, but after a period of 15 minutes she found that her anxiety reduced to 2. When this happened she stopped the task and agreed on a date and time to tackle the next task on her list until she completed all the tasks. Pam's hierarchy of feared situations is shown in Table 9.2.

you talk about your trauma or write about it, the better you will feel in the long term.

If as result of the trauma, you are avoiding places or activities, aim to tackle your avoidance using a step approach.

Before you undertake each new step it is important to stay in the situation until your anxiety subsides. If using a 1–10 scale and your anxiety goes down to 2 or 3 and stays there, this is an indication that you should move on to the next task. In many cases anxiety can take a while to reduce, so be patient.

If you are experiencing anger and/or irritability, try and recall the triggers for your reactions. They may be something other people say or do or the trigger may be anger which is directed at yourself. For example, Nick was furious at the driver who caused his car accident and after a while this fury started to extend to other drivers who he believed had poor driving skills; while Dee was angry at herself after being assaulted, because she chose to take a different route home just to get home more quickly. Normally Dee would not take this route because it wasn't well lit and was much quieter

TABLE 9.2   Pam's plan to tackle her fear of driving

Number	Anxiety rating on a scale of 0–10 prior to exposure	Situation
1	4	Standing next to the car with my hand on the bonnet
2	4.5	Sitting in the car in the driveway
3	5	Sitting in the car in the driveway with the engine turned on
4	6	Sitting in the passenger seat while my husband drives to the garden centre (20 minutes)
5	7	Driving to the garden centre while my husband sits in the passenger seat
6	7.5	Driving to my daughter's house and back with my husband in the passenger seat (1 hour)
7	8	Driving to my daughter's house using the motorway while my husband sits in the passenger seat
8	8.5	Driving to the supermarket on my own (half an hour)
9	9	Driving to my daughter's house on my own (using side roads)
10	9.5	Driving to my daughter's house using the motorway
11	10	Driving to the airport using the motorway to pick up my son

than the main road. Lastly, after being involved in a tube accident, Ben was furious at himself for having the symptoms of trauma. He described himself as 'weak and pathetic' for feeling this way and for not being able 'to dig himself out this hole'.

If you are able identify the possible triggers, you have a number of options to manage your reaction:

- Avoid the situations or people for the time being that contribute to you feeling angry.

- If you find your anger is directed at a partner or friend who has nothing to do with your trauma, explain to them that you are finding it hard to manage your temper because of your experience and that your reaction has nothing to do with them.

- Find different ways of releasing your anger from exercise to punching a cushion or attacking the weeds in the garden.

- Write down how you feel, express your anger in writing and be brutally honest, after all you are the only person who is going to read your account.

- Work through the thoughts that contribute to your anger, using the strategies outlined in Chapter 8 to challenge your anger-inducing thoughts. Ben used this technique to address his thoughts of feeling 'weak and pathetic' and not being able to 'dig himself out of a hole'. He used the internet to talk to others who had experienced traumas and found that they had experienced similar feelings and thoughts to him. This helped him to feel that he was not alone and to accept that his reactions were OK. He recognized that feeling 'pathetic or weak' was not helping to manage his recovery, rather it was hindering it. When he asked himself how he would react to another survivor of the tube accident who said that they were 'weak and pathetic', he acknowledged that he would react with great kindness towards them and tell them not to be hard on themselves. With this information he was able to tell himself that, 'My reaction to the trauma is pretty normal, I don't need to keep having a go at myself. I will dig myself out of this – it just takes time.'

- Use the spiral outlined in Chapter 8 to monitor your anger and to recognize how your anger spirals out of control. With practice and the strategies outlined, aim to stop your anger getting to the point where you cannot manage it.

Managing guilt associated with the trauma

The emotion of guilt is strongly associated with trauma. After the tube accident, Ben felt guilt about the accident in addition to feeling angry. After the accident he felt disorientated. He could not understand what had happened and his first instinct was to get out of the tube carriage and find a way out. He was successful but found out later that some of the people in the carriage were seriously hurt and that one man may not recover from his injuries. He began to feel guilty, believing that he should have done something to help others in the carriage. He felt that he should have stayed and helped, maybe in doing so he could have helped the one man with the serious injuries, maybe if he had been there his injuries would not have become life threatening. Likewise following a car accident, Gavin, the driver of the car, believed that he caused the injuries his brother had sustained whilst sitting in the back seat.

While Ben felt guilty because he should have stayed and helped, Gavin felt guilty because he didn't insist that his brother wore a seatbelt and felt 100 per cent responsible for his brother's injuries.

Having spoken to other people who have experienced traumas, Ben came to recognize that the situation he was in was 'special' in that it was so different to any other situations that he had experienced that the normal process of decision making did not apply. He didn't have time after the accident to think through the options; he only had seconds to make a decision and in any other situation in which his life wasn't at risk he may have made a different decision. Therefore he did not need to feel guilty for making a split-second decision in unusual circumstances. Instead of mentally beating himself up and dwelling on the accident, Ben let himself off the hook and came to recognize that he is not a bad person, rather a human being with a strong survival instinct.

Gavin, having spoken to a therapist friend of his, used the 'responsibility pie chart' to manage his guilt. His friend asked him to jot down the other factors that may have played a part in the accident. They are as follows:

1 The weather: it was raining heavily

2 The driver in front who stopped suddenly

3 The cyclist who swerved out in front of this driver causing him to break

4 Gavin's brother Adrian refused to wear his seat belt

5 Gavin's driving.

Having made the list Gavin then drew a circle and apportioned a realistic causal percentage to each item on the list. Figure 9.1 illustrates Gavin's response. Having allocated the percentages, Gavin realized that the part he played in the accident was minor; that factors 1–3 combined were the main contributors to the accident, not his driving. Using the responsibility pie chart helped Gavin to ease his feelings of guilt.

FIGURE 9.1   Responsibility pie chart

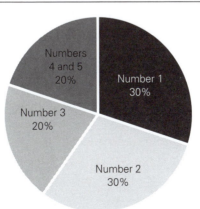

Grounding strategies

Grounding strategies are often applied to help individuals who have experience unwanted and emotional pain and flashbacks as a result of traumatic experiences. Essentially grounding is a form of distraction with the aim of shifting internal self-focus to an external focus. For example, following a serious assault abroad, Noah found that the strong sense of fear he experienced when he had come face to face with the assailant kept coming back. He believed that the experience was haunting him. He felt the fear in his stomach at odd times and he found it hard to know how to manage it. To distract his attention away from the fear, when at home he put his hands under a cold tap, and while at work where it was more difficult to use the bathroom whenever he needed to, he focused on the pictures of his dog on his i-Phone. Both these grounding strategies diverted his attention away from the fear to the external realm.

What to do if your recovery process is slow or at a standstill

If you find that you are taking a long time to get over the traumatic incident or notice that your symptoms are getting worse or you start to feel depressed (see Chapter 10 for information on symptoms) you may want to speak to your GP about getting help from a psychologist trained in cognitive behaviour therapy.

Chapter Ten
Conquering depression

Depression is a very common experience. The World Health Organization (WHO) states that depression affects 121 million people worldwide, while in the UK, research in psychological problems by MIND found that in 2007, 2.6 per cent of the population experienced depression. Many well-known figures have been reported to have suffered from depression, including Isaac Newton and Winston Churchill.

Depression is a debilitating and often an isolating and distressing experience. It impacts on how a person feels and the way they see themselves (often individuals view depression as sign of weaknesses), other people and the world in general. It can lead to trying physical symptoms such as poor energy, sleep patterns and concentration. It can last for a long time and is more than just 'feeling down'. The longer depression lasts, the more entrenched it can become. After a while it becomes harder and harder to pull yourself out of it and individuals can feel helpless or trapped. Also without any treatment – whether this is pharmacological or therapeutic – depression can reoccur. However, on a positive note depression does respond very well to cognitive behavioural self-help or therapy, or a combination of both. Understanding their depression helps individuals to manage it in a better way and specifically to recognize the early warning signs of future episodes.

Here we address the causes and symptoms of depression and the techniques that can be adopted to cope with and conquer the symptoms.

What constitutes depression?

The type, length and symptoms of depression a person experiences vary from person to person. One of the most common forms of depression is major depression. This is diagnosed by medical professionals if the person experiences some of the symptoms listed in Table 10.1 for at least two weeks.

Another form of depression is known as dysthymia. This is a more pervasive low mood that is often present for over two years. Finally, bipolar depression, previously known as manic depression, involves extremes of high, alternating with low moods and periods of more 'normal' moods.

While in Table 10.1 we outlined some of the more common signs, the table is by no means all inclusive. If you have other symptoms

TABLE 10.1   Common signs of depression

Low mood
A lack of interest and pleasure in activities in which you would normally find some enjoyment
A change in your sleep patterns, eg waking early
Either weight loss or gain
Feeling agitated or of being slowed down
Feeling worthless, experiencing low self-esteem or guilt
A lack of energy or fatigue
Trouble concentrating
Thoughts of suicide
Spiral of negative thinking, eg 'I'm worthless'
Other signs: despair, sadness, difficulty making decisions, irritability, low motivation, lack of interest in sex, unhappiness, self-criticism and numbness.

they may well be associated with depression. If you believe that you are feeling depressed do go to your GP or occupational health doctor to discuss your symptoms.

What causes depression?

The causes of depression are often multifaceted and initially viewing a cause in terms of internal versus external triggers can be helpful. There is evidence to suggest that there is a genetic component to depression, so having a family member who has experienced depression may make you more susceptible to developing it. Likewise a neurochemical imbalance in the brain can contribute to depression development and maintenance, as can a tendency towards negative thinking patterns. External causes can include an increase in work stress, financial problems, bereavement and divorce. In a recent study by the Elizabeth Finn Care charity researchers found that as a consequence of the recession, of the people who had lost their jobs recently, 71 per cent experienced symptoms of depression, while 51 per cent of those whose hours or salaries were cut also experienced symptoms of depression. Quite simply the recession has led to an increase in the chance of developing a depressive disorder.

In our work as psychologists we have seen a large number of people for therapy who are experiencing depression for a range of reasons which include a combination of internal and external causes.

Examples

Thomas

Thomas was referred for treatment by his GP after he complained of working long hours in IT; he was also having difficulty adjusting to his new manager of four months. During the assessment it became clear that there was a history of depression on his mother's side. As a child and teenager Thomas was very good in school, he achieved excellent results without trying too hard and his parents praised his excellent grades and questioned his less than excellent grades (any grade below an A). On leaving school Thomas went to work in the IT industry and did very well until the start of the recession. He enjoyed his job but as the recession deepened his company was taken over and to prove himself Thomas began to work longer hours. He began to feel tired, his team were demotivated as was he and it was proving hard to meet the targets set by his new manager. Thomas found that despite his perseverance in the post he and his team were not achieving what he thought they should. He began to think of himself as a failure. Unlike in childhood when it was easy to achieve good results, as an adult working under extreme pressure he was not achieving and meeting his high standards.

In tandem Thomas's home life began to suffer, he saw less of his children, and his wife became distant and complained that his priority was his work not his home. Thomas began to feel depressed and saw himself as a 'weak idiot' because he felt depressed and a failure who could not juggle his work and personal life. He took time off work, which seemed to make him feel worse. He felt tired and really couldn't be bothered to do anything around the house, which only served to reinforce his negative beliefs about himself. Ultimately he saw his GP, who recommended medication in combination with cognitive behavioural therapy.

Sara

After having time off for a serious back operation Sara returned to work in project management. She now had a new manager and team and found it hard to get back into the working pattern. Furthermore her manager seemed uninterested in supporting her. Initially Sara returned on a part-time basis, which she found beneficial. However, when she returned full-time her team took on the new challenge of a project, and with this came very long working hours. Sara found that she struggled to manage the hours and her back was painful due to having to sit at her desk for long periods; she found that she was irritable, her concentration was poor and her motivation was waning. Her sleep also suffered, she was waking during the night thinking of the project and at times she woke early and was unable to get back to sleep. During the working day she felt tired and worried about her ability to complete the project; overall she was finding it increasingly difficult to get all her work done during the day. She started to feel depressed about her situation.

In both the examples described above, external factors combined with internal ones led to Thomas and Sara feeling depressed. Thomas believed that he had let himself and his family down, while Sara felt let down by her employers and because she was living on her own she felt isolated with nobody to talk to.

Techniques to manage your depression

There are a number of very well researched strategies which serve to improve depressive symptoms. It is important that you read about all the techniques outlined in this chapter and aim to do as much as possible to kick-start managing the symptoms. You will find that making changes in one area can have a positive impact on your motivation to address another. We start off with the notion of getting back into the swing of things or reactivating your life.

Improving your activity levels

The founder of cognitive behavioural therapy, Aaron Beck, observed that individuals who feel depressed often lack belief in their ability to function well. In addition they lack enthusiasm and interest in activities they used to enjoy, for example going to the gym, reading, listening to music or playing with their children. As a result this lack of activity leads to a lack of enjoyment and satisfaction in their lives, which in turn makes them feel worse; low in energy, tired and more depressed. In other words, many depressed individuals often find themselves stuck in a vicious cycle of inactivity; the less they do, the less they want to do.

One of the key blocks to increasing activity levels is the lack of motivation or enthusiasm; this is not unusual but it will hinder your progress. Waiting for the motivation to do more or postponing doing more 'until you feel you want to' is counterproductive. If you feel depressed, the motivation will usually happen once you have engaged in the activities, not necessarily before you attempt them. You may want to think about increasing your activity in small steps and if possible get the support of family members or friends who

TABLE 10.2 Thomas's behavioural experiment

Activity	Negative thoughts about the activity	Realistic thoughts	Outcome
Going to gym	I can't be bothered, it won't help anyway	I don't know that it won't help, I'll give it a go	Went for half an hour, felt a bit better because I did something
Going out with my wife and kids to the park	I will only make my wife and kids miserable	Give it a go and see what happens	The kids seemed quite happy because I was there and at least I forgot about how I was feeling for a short time

can help motivate you. You can also treat planning your activities as a behavioural experiment. Test out whether doing more makes you feel better, consider how you feel before engaging in an activity that you think may make you feel better and work with the thoughts that block you from doing more. After you have completed the activity, review your progress. An example of Thomas's behavioural experiment is outlined in Table 10.2.

Planning your schedule helps to overcome apathy, can reduce negative thinking and the more you do the more you feel in control and able to tackle your depressive symptoms.

Developing an activation plan if you are depressed and not working

Ideally the activation plan needs to be as detailed as possible, planned in advance and consist of a mixture of activities and routine tasks which are realistic, specific and achievable in the time frame.

Tina, who was off work due to depression, recognized that staying in bed until lunch and then watching television in the afternoon was not helping her. Together with her partner she drew up a weekly plan of activities. Initially in her plan, she included activities which most probably would have been difficult to achieve (for example, attending three kick-boxing classes on a Monday, Tuesday and Wednesday night) and could have led to her to feeling discouraged to complete further tasks if she didn't manage to go on all three of the days. On discussion with her partner she made a list of activities which are more achievable. Her final first weekly schedule is outlined below:

Developing a plan if you are working and feeling depressed

In our experience, individuals who work and feel depressed often feel exhausted after work and go home and do very little. They put off tasks that need to be done around the house, see less of friends and engage less with partners and family. As discussed above this maintains the depressive symptoms; planning activities for the evening and weekends helps to counter exhaustion and makes people feel less depressed. Examples of planned evening and weekend activities include having a takeaway, going out for dinner, going for a walk, swim or to the gym, planning a holiday, cooking, reading a magazine, meeting a friend, going to an evening class and having a massage.

In summary the key factors to planning and engaging in activities and developing a schedule are:

- setting clear and specific tasks;
- setting realistic tasks;
- setting achievable tasks;
- combining routine tasks with pleasurable activities;
- valuing your accomplishments.

TABLE 10.3 Tina's weekly activity schedule

Time	Monday	Tuesday	Wednesday	Thursday	Friday	Saturday	Sunday
8am–10am	Get up and have breakfast	Get up and have breakfast	Get up and have breakfast	Get up and have breakfast	Get up and have breakfast	Get up and have breakfast	Get up and have breakfast
10am–12pm	Go for a 20 minute walk	Take the cat to the vet	Go for a 20 minute walk	Do the finances	Go for a 20 minute walk	Tidy the garden	Go for half hour swim
12pm–2pm	Catch up with e-mails	Tidy the garden	Clean out the spare room	Tidy the garden	Catch up with e-mails	Go food shopping	Meet up with Paul for lunch
2pm–4pm	Eat lunch and do household chores	Eat lunch and do household chores	Eat lunch and do household chores	Eat lunch and do household chores	Eat lunch and do household chores	Eat lunch and read newspaper	Meet up with Paul for lunch
4pm–6pm	Speak to Emma on the phone	Surf the internet	Speak to Mira on the phone	Go for therapy	Surf the internet	Surf the internet	Plan schedule for next week
6pm–8pm	Cook and eat dinner	Cook and eat dinner	Cook and eat dinner	Cook and eat dinner	Cook and eat dinner	Order a takeaway	Cook and eat dinner
8pm–10pm	Watch a film	Watch favourite TV serial	Watch TV	Phone Paula and e-mail David	Play board games with Petra	Watch a film	Play board games with Petra
10pm–12am	Prepare for bed	Prepare for bed	Prepare for bed	Prepare for bed	Prepare for bed	Prepare for bed	Prepare for bed

Working with your negative thoughts

In addition to building up activity levels, identifying and challenging NATs is an important component of depression. Aaron Beck suggested that individuals who are depressed often hold increasingly negative/harsh thoughts about themselves, their current experiences and their future. Some examples of this negative triad follow:

Negative thoughts about self: 'I'm useless, I'm rubbish, I'm not good enough, I can't deal with this, and I'm messing everything up because I'm so tired.'

Negative thoughts about your current experience: 'There must be something wrong with me to get so depressed; what have I done to feel so bad? Nobody understands how I feel.'

Negative thoughts about your future: 'I'm never going to get better, there is no end in sight; my partner will leave me before long, he must be so frustrated with me; my manager must be wondering what is wrong with me, he is bound to tell HR to make me redundant.

In Chapter 2 we outlined how to work with negative thoughts. To recap, you need to get into the habit of writing down your negative thoughts as soon as they pop into your mind, and then try to link them to the thinking errors before using the automatic thought form to work through your negative thoughts. If you have recognized that core beliefs are affecting your depression, refer back to the exercises in the same chapter.

How to stop beating yourself up

If you find that you are also beating yourself up for feeling depressed, tired or unmotivated, adapt the list outlined in Chapter 6, which focuses on the reasons why not to worry. Make a new heading entitled 'The reasons why I don't need to beat myself up' and list 3–6 reasons why beating yourself up is unhelpful. If you are having problems thinking of some good reasons ask yourself the following questions:

- Is there any advantage to beating myself up?
- What are the short- and long-term consequences of beating myself up?

- How does beating myself up affect me?
- Is it helping me to manage my depression?
- What would I say to a friend who was doing the same thing?

Keep the list at hand and read it every day.

Problem solving

Often the experience of depression can have an impact on the ability to problem solve. Individuals who feel depressed and hopeless can struggle to effectively problem solve and make decisions. Using the PRACTICE model (see Appendix E) is an effective way of dealing with both small and large problems and can help individuals feel more in control of their depression.

Decision making

Making decisions can be tiring if you are feeling depressed and individuals often worry that the decisions they make will be the wrong ones, which in turn stops them from making any decisions. If you are feeling severely depressed a quick rule of thumb is to try not to make any life-changing decisions such as moving jobs until your depression has lifted a little, as when you start to feel better your clarity of thinking will improve. Otherwise a structured format to making decisions can help to overcome this debilitating process. Appendix I is a blank form which supports effective decision making, focusing on the pros and cons of making decisions together with looking at the short- and long-term implications of every option.

Working with low self-esteem/worth

Low self-esteem is commonly associated with depression. In the section on negative thoughts noted earlier, we list some of the negative self-beliefs associated with depression such as 'I'm useless' or 'I'm rubbish'. These are essentially labels which make you feel worse. If you tell yourself that you are useless the likelihood is that you will look for any evidence to support this notion and most probably discount any evidence that suggests the opposite. This just reinforces the label or the idea and makes you feel more depressed.

To counter low self-esteem, in Chapter 2 we focused on how to work with labels in the section on core beliefs and then in Chapter 7 we addressed the techniques used to develop self-acceptance as opposed to working on self-esteem, which involves not rating ourselves as a whole, rather only rating our behaviours, thoughts or feelings.

Ivan saw himself as failure in his new managerial role; he was struggling to manage his team of six, and to get on top of his work-load. In his mind he had an idea of how a manager 'should perform' and he believed his performance fell short of his expectations. When questioned Ivan admitted that he thought of himself as a total 'no hoper'. To illustrate how obstructive this label is, his therapist drew three circles (see Figure 10.1). The first circle with crosses represents a person who is a total 'no hoper' – every cross represents a form of failure – while the second circle represents a person who is perfect – every tick represents perfection – while the last circle represents a person who is fallible, one who has a mix of traits, including neutral and average traits. On deliberation Ivan acknowledged that he did fall into the last circle.

FIGURE 10.1   The three circles

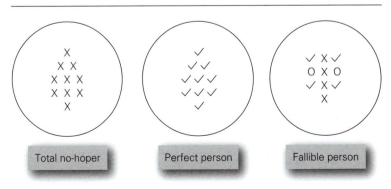

Total no-hoper   Perfect person   Fallible person

His therapist then asked him to find and jot down some evidence to refute the idea that he was a total failure. Although he struggled, Ivan was able to make a list of seven points which weakened his conviction in the idea that he was a 'no hoper'. He then went on to work on the application of self-acceptance with his therapist.

Listing the good things that happened each day

When feeling depressed individuals can forget or gloss over the good things that happened each day; instead things that didn't go well or general concerns seem more prominent. In order to counter the emphasis on negativity we recommend making a list of the positive things that happened during the day, such as: getting a seat on the train; reading an interesting article; someone smiling at you; eating a delicious meal; or playing with your children or pets. Aim to reread the list regularly.

Improving sleep patterns

For some people another casualty of depression is poor sleep, for example trouble falling asleep, waking during the night or very early in the morning and then having problems falling back to sleep. Research into improving sleeping patterns has highlighted the following dos and don'ts to aid sleep:

- Aim to go to bed and wake up at the same time every day of the week.

- Make a list of anything that is troubling you before you go to bed to clear your mind of work and personal issues.

- If you wake up and cannot sleep, get up and do something boring and then when you are tired go back to bed. Don't lie awake worrying about the fact that you are awake.

- Turn your alarm clock round, don't look at it when you wake up early. Looking at the clock only reminds you that you are awake at wrong times and it can trigger renewed thinking.

- Take time to prepare yourself for bed. If possible take up to an hour; you can have a bath or listen to music. Don't do anything mentally taxing in that time, try to switch off and relax.

- Aim not to exercise or eat a big meal late, both can inhibit sleeping.

Reducing the chances of future depressive episodes

To reduce the chances of experiencing another depressive episode, aim to think back to the start of your depression. Can you determine what your early warning signs are? Was it feeling anxious, feeling tearful, having trouble sleeping or overthinking? Did a combination of stressful events which you could not control make you feel low and then that spiralled into depression? If you are having trouble isolating the initial signs, speak to a family member or friend if you can and ask them if they noticed any changes in your behaviour or attitude?

Make a list of these early warning signs and don't ignore them. Aim to deal with the triggers as soon as they happen. Either use the strategies in this book, or see your doctor to discuss the possibility of taking medication or/and have some cognitive behavioural therapy.

Seek help

If at any time you have suicidal thoughts or harm yourself (for example, deliberately cutting your arms or legs) seek help from your GP as soon as possible. If you struggle going on your own take your partner or a good friend.

Chapter Eleven
Managing workplace bullying

Research and public awareness into bullying has increased significantly in the past decade. In 2004 Noreen Tehrani found in a study of 165 care professionals that over a two-year period 40 per cent of employees had been bullied, while 68 per cent had seen bullying taking place. More recently in the United States, the Workplace Bullying Institute estimated that 35 per cent of the US employees (that is 53.5 million people) had experienced bullying and that while both men and women bully, the majority of bullying was same-sex bullying.

Here we concentrate on what constitutes bullying, before addressing strategies aimed at managing bullying in the short and long term.

What is bullying?

Bullying is an aggressive and unwanted form of behavior which often includes physical and/or verbal abuse. Being bullied over time can undermine confidence and lead to other problems. Bullying can be 'downward' when managers bully, 'horizontal' when employees bully others at the same level, or 'upward' when managers are bullied by their staff.

What constitutes bullying?

There is a distinction between indirect and direct bulling. The first category includes isolating employees and controlling or manipulating the information received by an employee. The second category includes making offensive remarks, discrediting the person's professional reputation and undervaluing the person's role. The most common form of bullying behaviour includes unfair criticism followed by intimidation, unpleasant remarks, public humiliation, malicious gossip, being ignored and making threats. Other forms include moving the goalposts, setting impossible deadlines, preventing access to professional development opportunities, and taking responsibilities away from individuals.

The impact of bullying

Regardless of the type of bullying experienced, this behaviour can lead to serious psychological ill health and have a bearing on team morale, efficiency and reduced job satisfaction. From a psychological perspective, bullying can heighten stress levels, lead to low self-confidence, worry, tension, fatigue, anxiety, depression and even symptoms of post-traumatic disorder such as a tendency to think about or picture the bullying episode when you don't want to, dreaming about it, feeling tense or irritable, being jumpy and feeling guilty.

Maria

Maria described being 'picked on by her boss.' She sat in an open plan office with her boss next to her. Her boss talked in a very loud voice and regularly berated Maria's reports and her working style. Maria noticed that she didn't do this to the other team members and favoured the two men in the team. Initially Maria ignored her behaviour, but after a period of two months she found that she lacked motivation in work and 'didn't feel like going in'. Her boss picked up on her lack of motivation and criticised her for it, Maria's colleagues noticed the bullying and urged her to talk to her boss or report it to HR.

Maria now felt under pressure 'to do something constructive about this' but she didn't want to talk to her boss, who had a bad temper, and she felt guilty about talking to HR. She began to have problems falling asleep, her concentration was poor which led to some mistakes in her work, she felt tense and tearful and considered looking for another job in the company but was worried that her boss would either give her a bad reference or not let her leave the department.

Ross

Ross, a senior manager, described feeling helpless and depressed following a six-month period of being bullied by one of his team who was furious when Ross addressed his poor attendance. The employee spread malicious gossip about his personal life, accused him in an underhand manner of bullying female team members and commented negatively on his dress sense. Ross attempted to address the bullying with the employee but with little success. The bully was a popular member of the team who Ross believed was supported by the other team members; they found his comments funny and often sniggered when Ross walked past.

Embarrassed at being bullied and talking to HR, Ross tried to ignore it, hoping that it would end. However, he found that his confidence was affected, so began to feel miserable and low. He 'couldn't think straight', believed that he was an 'idiot' who couldn't manage himself let alone a team, and described 'feeling like a rat trapped in a small cage, with no way out'.

The antecedents to bullying

In addition to focusing on what bullying involves and its effect on people, researchers have also tried to address the contextual factors within organizations which may facilitate a culture of bullying. It has been citied that changes within organizations such as staff shortages, role conflicts, restructuring, job uncertainty, increase in workload, stress, difficult relationships, imbalances in power and lack of effective organizational bullying policies can provide a breeding ground for bullying.

Interventions to resolve and prevent bullying

Ignoring bullying behaviour and hoping it will improve is not the best strategy to manage bullies, as bullies often interpret the perceived passivity from their victims as a green light to intensify their bullying tactics. Taking a proactive stance towards bullying works best.

Keep a record of your bullies' behaviour, note down the date, what they said, how you felt and, if applicable, how you responded, who else was there (if anyone) and where you were.

Confronting the bully can work. If you are nervous confronting your bully, practise what you are going to say, or write it down and then suggest a meeting with the bully in a quiet place. Use the assertion skills outlined in the next chapter. Remember both verbal and nonverbal communication is important. If you need to practise your assertion skills, do so in advance. When talking to the bully keep your voice steady and be direct and to the point; do not allow yourself to get side-tracked. Keep a written record of what was said. If the bully's behaviour does not change after a period of time, aim to repeat the process. If you have confronted your bully two or three times and the bullying continues seek other support.

Get support: do talk to trusted work colleagues, friends and family. Also if you have confronted your bully and their behaviour continues, speak to your manager, the head of the department and/or HR.

Maria tackles her bully

Maria made the decision to confront her bully; she practiced what she was going to say and then asked to see her boss in a side room. She sat down with her and initiated the conversation. She picked on the two most recent incidents of bullying and used the broken record technique (to learn about this strategy see Chapter 12) to communicate her message. She also stated that unless the bullying behaviour stopped now, she would speak to her manager's manager and to HR. Her bully backed down, she stopped criticizing her work and style of working and as result Maria's confidence slowly improved.

Remember that companies are obliged to act when they are aware of an employee bullying others. Do not be afraid to do so. It's possible that HR are already aware of that person's behaviour and your experience will enable HR to tackle the bullying using the evidence they now have. If you feel isolated, recognize that the bullying has affected you psychologically and find yourself struggling to manage work, try to find support via coaching or therapy.

Look after yourself. In our experience bullying can have serious ramifications not only on your professional life but also on your personal life. If you recognize that your behaviour and attitude to work and your personal life have changed as a result of the bullying, aim to deal with the consequences of the bullying. For example, if you notice that you are worrying more, thinking about the bullying in more depth than need be, or blaming yourself, write down how you are feeling. Keeping a diary can be therapeutic. Remind yourself that worrying about the situation or blaming yourself will only make you feel worse. Use the techniques in the chapters in this book to address your concerns. Also make sure you look after yourself outside work: see friends or go and see a film, try to fill your evenings and weekends with activities you enjoy.

Ultimately to reduce the chances of bullying happening within organizations, awareness of bullying needs to be high on the organizational agenda together with the implementation of anti-bullying polices.

Chapter Twelve
Developing assertiveness techniques

Communicating in an assertive manner is the key to building and maintaining respectful relationships in professional and personal spheres. Assertive behaviour is also linked to increased self-confidence, a sense of control and improved self-esteem. One of the 'concerns' often voiced by individuals about assertion is that it is the same as aggression, but this is completely untrue. Assertive behaviour involves standing up for yourself, asking for what you want, and giving constructive feedback in a calm manner without resorting to aggression. This behaviour leads to a win-win situation. This is very different to aggressive behaviour. Aggressive responses involve demanding what you want: the tone of voice is very different, often cold and even sarcastic, the voice may be raised, they may shout and the content of the communication does not allow for negotiation or feedback. In fact it can lead to negative consequences outlined earlier and a sense of feeling violated. In addition to assertive and aggressive behaviours the other two styles of behaviours adopted by people include passive and passive-aggressive behaviours.

The four styles of behaviour and their identifiable characteristics

Assertive style

An assertive style involves: being relaxed and speaking in a steady firm tone without raising your voice; expressing your emotions either verbally or non-verbally (for example, smiling); requesting feedback if appropriate to maintain a collaborative stance, using 'I' statements; taking on board and accepting constructive criticism; using open questions; and tackling problems in a shared, solution-focused manner.

Some assertive statements include:

- I feel hurt because you have put me down in front of the manager.
- Let's talk about this next week when we have more time.
- How can we deal with this?
- I appreciate that you are upset; however, we do need to resolve this. We can take a break and then talk about this over coffee.

Aggressive style

An aggressive style involves: dominating conversations, pointing and a clenched fist; invading one's personal space; talking fast or in a cold, clipped, sarcastic or intimidating manner; using words such as 'should' or 'must' or threatening others; leaving no room for negotiation. This can leave the recipient feeling attacked, got at and angry.

Some aggressive statements include:

- That is a really ineffectual way of doing that.
- You really should be more careful, haven't you learnt anything yet?
- You are behaving like a child, not an adult; Grow up!
- Why can't you grasp a simple concept like that?

Passive style

A passive style includes not saying what you think and feel; the reasons for this can be varied (for example, being worried that you will upset the other person or low self-esteem). Individuals who behave passively often use the phrases, 'maybe', 'it doesn't matter' and 'sort of'. They can take a long time to say something and in addition often apologize for what they are saying. They can look away when talking, shrug, wring their hands or put their hand over their mouth so it's hard to understand what they are saying.

Some passive statements include:

- I'm really sorry to ask you to do this.

- Look I don't like to interfere.

- I'm not really very good at using spreadsheets, pretty useless, as with a lot of things.

- I know you are busy, I'll come back later.

Passive-aggressive style

A passive-aggressive style includes: being manipulative, irritable, sullen and angry; having a low frustration tolerance; finding it difficult to express one's emotions; not doing what you are asked to do in a work situation or performing the task slowly to 'express' your displeasure; feeling resentful; procrastinating; not taking responsibility; and withholding doing tasks. This type of behaviour often leaves its recipients feeling let down, confused, hurt or angry.

Some passive aggressive statements incude:

- I'll do that later.

- No you didn't ask me to that.

- My work colleagues are against me.

- He doesn't deserve that pay rise.

Assertive language, behaviour and techniques

Assertion consists of three main components: non-verbal behaviour, language and specific techniques. To combine these elements in your communication requires practice and a positive attitude to assertion. Think of assertion as a skill that needs to be acquired and developed over time, much like learning to drive. Overall assertive behaviour fosters self-confidence and resilience.

Non-verbal behaviour includes: maintaining eye contact without staring; keeping your voice steady and measured, jaw relaxed and your posture and facial expressions consistent with the message you are delivering. In other words if you are telling someone that you are annoyed with their behaviour it would be appropriate to frown.

Language includes: using 'I' statements such as 'I think' and 'I feel'; omitting 'shoulds' and musts', instead asking (for example, 'We could aim to...'); using open questions such as, 'What do you think?;' being upfront and saying 'no' if appropriate and adding your reason(s) for doing so; being open to working collaboratively to resolve issues and develop solutions (for example, 'How would you like to resolve this issue?').

Specific techniques

The broken record

This involves stating what you think and/or feel without getting sidelined into another argument. It involves repeating want you want to say until you are heard.

Manager:	Paul doesn't have time to do this, so I want you to take it over and get it finished and on my desk by 6pm today.
Stewart:	I do have other work that needs to be completed by the end of today, so I'm afraid I won't have time to do this job by the end of today.

Manager: Well I want you to drop that and do this.

Stewart: I can't drop the other work. I need to complete it by the
            end of the day and therefore won't be able to do the job
            you want me to do.

Fogging

This involves standing up for yourself in the face of criticism, which
can often be harsh, by acknowledging your mistake. By doing this
you are disempowering your critic in a self-confident manner.

Manager: You keep handing in work late all the time.

David: Yes I know this work is late, my apologies. However,
            the last time this happened was two months ago;
            it doesn't happen 'all the time'.

Finding a workable solution

This focuses on developing a win-win solution.

Manager: This project must be on my desk by Monday 9 am.
            Can you come in over the weekend to finish it?

Nanette: No, I'm away this weekend; however, I can stay late
            tonight and come in an hour early tomorrow morning to
            complete it.

Negative enquiry

This entails asking for specific constructive feedback when another
person gives general unconstructive feedback.

Team member: I don't see how you will manage that presentation
              on your own; you are not very good at giving
              presentations

Mark: What do you think my skills deficits are in this area?

Negative feeling assertion

This requires expressing clearly how you feel, how the other person's behaviour impacts on you and how you want the other person's behaviour to change. For example: 'When you put down my efforts in front of others I feel hurt, so from now on I want you to stop doing that.'

Discrepancy assertion

This involves pointing out the inconsistencies in other people's comments. For example: 'Michael when I asked you to complete the spreadsheet you told me that you would do it later. It's now 6 pm and you are preparing to leave the office and the spreadsheet is not completed. Can you explain to me what has happened?'

Setting clear boundaries

This involves creating boundaries that work for you and if need be reminding others of them. For example, when you manager calls you when you are at home: 'Please do not phone me at home again. I'm not well and not up to talking about work until I'm back in the office.'

Asking for time

If you need time to consider a point raised do ask for it. For example: 'I need time to think about the restructuring, I will get back to you by 5 pm.'

Assertiveness rights

Finally, remember that being assertive with people whether they are work colleagues or friends is acceptable; it is not rude or hurtful, rather it is your right to be assertive in an honest and clear manner. As human beings we have assertiveness rights, which are (adapted from Smith, 1975):

- the right to say no;
- the right not to justify one's behaviour;
- the right to make mistakes;
- the right to state one's own needs;
- the right to be oneself;
- the right to change one's mind;
- the right to take responsibility for one's own actions;
- the right not to understand.

In addition, others have modified this list to include the following employee rights (Centre for Stress Management, 2005):

- the right to fulfil one's potential;
- the right to give constructive criticism to other employees;
- the right to look after oneself and take time off without feeling guilty or pressurized to get back to work;
- the right to ask for support and advice;
- the right to training and to learn new skills;
- the right to receive acknowledgement for one's work;
- the right to be heard by mangers and other staff;
- the right to ask for time if needed;
- the right to be consulted on matters that impact on oneself;
- the right to say no to unreasonable requests;
- the right to ask for extra time;
- the right to make mistakes;
- the right to be treated with respect.

Chapter Thirteen
Developing time-management skills and overcoming procrastination

Good time managememt

Good time management is an important skill for both work and personal life. It helps efficiency in both domains, freeing us up for more enjoyable activities. Poor time management is a major cause of stress, especially at work. Not only do we let ourselves down, we let others down with whom we are working on projects and tasks. We have placed this chapter after Chapter 12 intentionally – to be a good time manager you need to be assertive. This is crucial, otherwise it is too easy to take on too many tasks, especially if you are a people pleaser.

Listing your goals

Setting goals is important, and when doing so think about goals that are specific and achievable within the time frame that you have.

At the start of each week, make a list of your goals and targets, and prioritize them. Revise the list daily, as necessary, and regularly refer to it. Some laptops and computers have a 'sticky notes' facility where you can make your list and it is visible on your screen 24/7. Although this may seem rather a tough approach for you to take, being reminded of your goals and target for the week helps to maintain focus.

Spend time planning

Spend only an appropriate amount of time planning your workload or project. Often people with strong perfectionist beliefs such as 'I must perform well' may create high levels of anxiety in themselves and over-plan and over-prepare. At the start of a task it is a good idea to consider what would be a sensible amount of time for your planning stage. If in doubt you could discuss this with a colleague or your supervisor or manager.

One task at a time

To avoid making errors, doing one task at a time can often be helpful. This is dependent on the main task you need to focus on. In addition you need to allow extra time for the unexpected, and be realistic about how much work you and your colleagues can do.

Learn to say no

When being asked to take on a time-consuming task or project, avoid automatically saying yes to this request. It is important to ask yourself whether you really need to agree to the request being asked. If in doubt, you could ask for time before you reach a decision. Use assertiveness skills; say no when necessary.

Dealing with mail and e-mails

Tackle incoming postal mail and/or e-mails as soon as you open them if possible. If under pressure, consider prioritizing them and deal with the unimportant post or e-mails later. Some people find it helpful and less distracting not to download e-mails or log in until later in the day though this is not always practical.

Prepare meetings and calls

Prepare for meetings, including telephone or video conference meetings, and list items you wish to discuss. If possible, group outgoing telephone calls together.

Overcoming procrastination

To overcome procrastination we need to introduce some theory to explain why we procrastinate. Michael Neenan (2012) describes procrastination as, 'putting off until later what our better judgement tells us ought (preferably) to be done now, thereby incurring unwanted consequences through such dilatory behavior'. The 'putting off' occurs because the person is actively seeking more interesting or pleasurable activities to engage in rather than experiencing 'now' the discomfort or difficulty associated with doing the avoided tasks. Procrastination could also be considered as an anxiety-reducing behaviour which does not help the person to achieve their main goal(s) or targets.

Procrastination is different to planned delay in which there may be good reasons to postpone immediate work on a task or project such as checking out relevant data or seeking advice, or clarifying some aspect of a project. It is not correct to dismiss procrastination as 'laziness', as laziness involves unwillingness to exert yourself, while the former involves doing other things for the sake of it, in order to avoid getting on with the tasks you have prioritized.

Consider the last time you deferred starting or working on a project; what did you do instead? Did you do one of the following activities?

- cleaning and tidying your desk;
- dusting or tidying your room or computer screen;
- cleaning the kitchen floor;
- washing the windows;
- cutting the grass;
- weeding the garden;
- cleaning the car;
- talking to distant relatives;
- deleting unwanted e-mails;
- responding to unimportant e-mails;
- tidying up computer folders;

- surfing the internet;

- playing computer games;

- spending an inordinate amount of time making a priority list;

- spending days preparing the work by obtaining yet more background information;

- tidying the filing system;

- doing the unimportant jobs in the in-tray;

- answering unnecessary telephone calls;

- consuming more drinks, food or cigarettes than usual;

- whinging to colleagues about the amount of work you have;

- blaming your boss or others;

- telling others that you work best at the eleventh hour (or even later!).

Did you do one or more of the above? The list covers the type of procrastinating behaviours that people have reported doing when not focusing on the important task in hand.

Why do we procrastinate?

Let's consider why you procrastinated. Figure 13.1 illustrates what happens when a person procrastinates. As soon as a person has an important task to undertake that they believe or perceive they 'must' do well at, then their stress and anxiety levels usually rise. However, when they start distracting themselves with displacement behaviour such as deleting unwanted e-mails or tidying up their desk, their stress levels temporarily decrease. This is like a quick fix similar to comfort eating, smoking a cigarette or drinking a glass of wine. It takes the edge off how the person feels. As can be seen in Figure 13.1, after a period of time when they start to refocus on the important project or task, their stress and anxiety levels rise even higher than before when they realize they have less time to complete it.

FIGURE 13.1   Procrastination chart

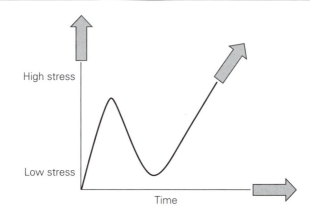

SOURCE: Cooper and Palmer, 2010

If you wish to overcome your procrastinating behaviours it is crucial that you recognize that you are doing something that is not focused on achieving your main goal(s) relating to the task or project. If you look at Figure 13.1 the unhelpful goal-blocking thoughts you have that initially cause your stress and anxiety to increase on the first part of the curve are the ones you need to tackle and modify. The thoughts and feelings that come afterwards are usually less important. Let's use the ABCDE model to illustrate John's problem:

- Activating event: Important work project to start work on.

- Beliefs: I must perform well (intermediate belief – rule). If I perform badly my colleagues will think I'm a failure (intermediate belief – negative underlying assumption). I'm a failure (core belief).

- Consequences: High anxiety; procrastinates (does not focus on project); plays a computer game.

Often perfectionists are reluctant to start a task or project due to fear of failure and anxiety about a less than perfect product, so John's experience is quite common. Once the key beliefs have been recognized, the next stage is for John to challenge and examine his thoughts and modify them. This stage in the ABCDE model is known as 'D' for disputation.

- Disputation: It's strongly preferable to perform well but realistically I don't have to (intermediate belief – flexible rule). If I perform badly my colleagues are unlikely to rate me based on one project (intermediate belief – more realistic underlying assumption). I'm fallible (new more helpful core belief).

- Effective new approach: makes a priority list of tasks and starts on project.

The usual behavioural time management techniques and strategies are less effective if a person has a psychological block to start a project, especially if they become anxious and procrastinate. The application of the psychological ABCDE model assists in exploring which blocks to change and how to overcome them.

Not all procrastination is due to raised stress and anxiety levels. If John found the preparation for the project tedious and boring he may still have procrastinated. The goal-blocking beliefs are likely to be different in these circumstances. For example, 'I can't stand doing tedious tasks' and 'I must enjoy myself.' Therefore the two beliefs 'I can't-stand-it-itis' and the rule belief should be challenged and modified. For example, 'I don't like it but I can stand it. It won't kill me!' and 'I don't have to enjoy myself all the time, although it's preferable to do so.'

Six fundamental procrastination styles

There are six main procrastination styles:

- perfectionism,
- the dreamer,
- the worrier,
- the defier,
- the crisis-maker,
- the overdoer.

Do you recognize any of them in yourself? If so, it is worth considering the beliefs you may have associated with them.

Chapter Fourteen
Dealing with difficult people

Dealing with difficult friends, family and colleagues can be quite challenging. You can feel guilty, undermined and manipulated when in a relationship with a difficult person. Often they have an ability to make you believe that you are in the wrong when in fact they are openly or subtly abusing you. In this final chapter we want to highlight some of the skills covered so far in this book that may help you to take a more proactive approach.

In Chapter 12 we discussed four main behavioural styles:

- assertive behaviours,
- aggressive behaviours,
- passive behaviours,
- passive-aggressive behaviours.

Dealing with people demonstrating an assertive style of behaviour is usually straightforward as they will respect you and your own needs. However, the other behavioural styles can be quite disruptive within work and personal relationships. The key assertion techniques (see pages 142–44) to use when dealing with difficult people who are being aggressive, passive or passive-aggressive are:

- the broken record;
- fogging;
- finding a workable solution;
- negative enquiry;
- negative feeling assertion;

- discrepancy assertion;
- setting clear boundaries;
- asking for time.

It is important to remain assertive yourself even if you are finding the situation with a demanding and manipulative manager or colleague challenging.

The three-step model of assertion

The three-step model is particularly useful when dealing with demanding and difficult people. This model allows you to make your point in an assertive manner, without becoming overly emotional and distressed, remaining focused on your wishes and goals without being offensive.

- Step 1: Actively listen to what the other person is saying and demonstrate to the other that you have heard and understood what they have said.
- Step 2: Say what you think and feel. (A good linking word to use here between step 1 and 2 is 'however'.)
- Step 3: Say what you want to happen. (A good linking word to use between step 2 and 3 is 'and'.)

Assertiveness skills are not always recommended, because their use by some people can increase the likelihood of violence occurring or because an employer may use their being deployed as an excuse to dismiss the person. In these situations an alternative course of action may be necessary.

A real example illustrating the three-step model with a demanding 'friend' is:

- Step 1: It would be nice to go out this evening.
- Step 2: However, I need to prepare for my work tomorrow.
- Step 3: And so I think I'll stay in this on this occasion.

A work example with a manipulative colleague is:

- Step 1: I realize this is important to you. I would really like to take on this extra project.
- Step 2: However, I need to complete the other project first before starting on this new project as my deadline is the end of this month.
- Step 3: And I do appreciate you considering me to work with you on this new project. Let's see what I can do next month.

These examples demonstrate how assertiveness skills can be applied to demanding and/or manipulative people.

Psychological blocks to dealing with difficult people

Even though you may use the three-step model of assertion, dealing with difficult people can trigger a range of beliefs and emotions which can sometimes hinder you in dealing constructively with the person concerned. In this section we will include a few examples of beliefs that may need examining and modifying.

Let's take an example of a manager who is demanding that Jane should work late to finish off a task. However, she has already agreed to take her mother out to the cinema. Difficult managers can get into the habit of making these demands. So preparing for the next time it happens is one strategy to deal with it. The ABCDE framework is illustrated below.

- Activating event: Manager who is demanding that an employee should work late to finish off a task.

- Beliefs: I should stay at work to finish this task (intermediate belief: a rule). If I don't stay on at work he (the manager) will think I'm useless (intermediate belief: negative underlying assumption). I'm useless (negative core belief).

- Consequences: Anxiety, guilt, avoidance of tackling the issue, considering cancelling the arrangement with mother and working late.

The next stage is dealing with the thinking that currently is likely to lead to Jane working late and not going out with her mother as planned. As the manager has asked her to stay late on a number of occasions, she has already prepared how to tackle her thinking.

- Disputation: Although my manager wants me to stay at work to finish a task, I don't have to. I can go home on time if I so wish (intermediate belief: flexible rule). If I don't stay on at work he (the manager) may have his own opinion of me but I don't have to agree with it (intermediate belief: realistic negative underlying assumption). I'm a good worker most of the time (realistic core belief).

- Effective: New approach. Informs manager she has a prior arrangement; does not beat herself up; suggests to manager that if she focuses on the task first thing the next morning she will probably have it finished by 10.15am.

The three-step model of assertion and the cognitive behavioural ABCDE models can work together to enable a person to remain focused and deal with their emotions of anxiety and guilt that often get triggered by difficult or challenging people. Hopefully a win-win result is possible but this is not always so. With some of our clients they have found that being consistently more assertive with difficult people often wins their respect and increases their own self-respect. Sometimes so-called difficult people become easier to handle and in fact you come to realize that the most difficult person to handle was yourself!

Appendix A
A blank automatic thought form

Situation	Your negative thoughts about the situation	Your feelings and physical responses	Develop realistic thoughts	Effective new way of dealing with the situation
A	B	C	D	E

Appendix B
Coping imagery

Step 1: Outline the situation that you imagine you will find difficult to manage

_____

_____

↓

Step 2: Outline the critical aspects of the situation which you find difficult

_____

_____

↓

Step 3: Consider the strategies you need to manage the situation adequately

_____

_____

↓

Step 4: Visualize yourself coping with the situation using the strategies outlined above. Repeat this visualization on a regular basis, preferably daily

Appendix C
A blank panic management form

Situation/trigger for my worry	Your response (eg heart racing, dizziness, feeling faint)	Your negative thoughts about your response	Your realistic thoughts

Appendix D
A blank worry form

Trigger for my worry	My worries	Impact of my worry on my feelings and/or actions	Logical reassessment of my worries

Appendix E
A blank PRACTICE solutions form

STEP 1: PROBLEM IDENTIFICATION
What is the problem, issue or concern? What would you like to change?
Are there exceptions when it is not a problem? How will we know if the situation has improved?

STEP 2: REALISTIC and RELEVANT GOALS DEVELOPED
What do you want to achieve? Consider developing SMART Goals (eg Specific, Measurable, Achievable, Realistic, Timebound goal(s))

STEP 3: ALTERNATIVE SOLUTIONS GENERATED
What are your options? Write down possible ways of reaching your goals.

STEP 4: CONSIDER THE CONSEQUENCES
What could happen? How useful is each possible solution? Weigh up the pros and cons. Use a usefulness rating scale: 1–10.

STEP 5: TARGET MOST FEASIBLE SOLUTION(S)
Choose the most feasible solution(s).

STEP 6: IMPLEMENTATION OF CHOSEN SOLUTION(S)
Break down the solution into manageable steps. Now go and do it.

STEP 7: EVALUATION
How successful was it? Use a rating 'success' scale 1–10. Focus on your achievement. What can you learn from it?

Appendix F
Proactive approach to worrying

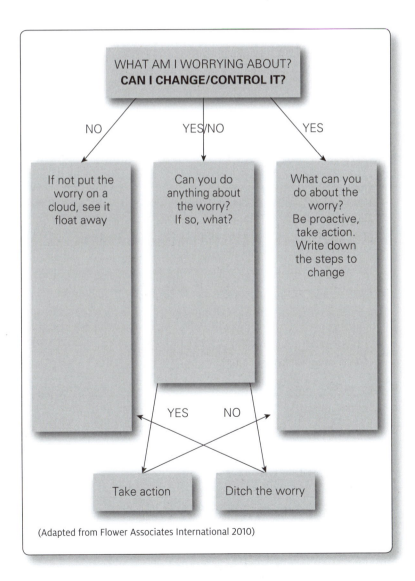

WHAT AM I WORRYING ABOUT?
CAN I CHANGE/CONTROL IT?

NO — If not put the worry on a cloud, see it float away

YES/NO — Can you do anything about the worry? If so, what?

YES — What can you do about the worry? Be proactive, take action. Write down the steps to change

YES   NO

Take action   Ditch the worry

(Adapted from Flower Associates International 2010)

Appendix G
Thinking in extremes continuum

My extreme thinking

_____

_____

_____

X _____ X
| |
↓   ↓

Impact of this type   Impact of this type
of thinking   of thinking

_____   _____

_____   _____

_____   _____

                    Middle ground
          X ←——————————————————→ X

←——→

                    |
                    ↓

Resilient thinking:

_____

_____

_____

Appendix H
A blank personal anger triggers and reactions form

Personal anger triggers and my reaction(s)

Anger trigger	My reaction to this trigger, including my thoughts, actions and physiological responses

Appendix I
A decision form

Decision to be made

_____

_____

Pros

1.

_____

_____

Short-term consequences

_____

_____

Long-term consequences

_____

_____

2.

_____

_____

Short-term consequences

_____

_____

Long-term consequences

_____

_____

Cons

1.

_____

_____

Short-term consequences

_____

_____

Long-term consequences

_____

_____

2.

_____

_____

Short-term consequences

_____

_____

Long-term consequences

_____

_____

Bibliography

Chapter 2

Dryden, W., Neenan, M. and Yankura, M. (1999) *Counselling Individuals: A Rational Emotive Behavioural Handbook*, 3rd edition. London: Whurr.

Greenberger, D. and Padesky, C.A. (1995) *Mind Over Mood: A cognitive therapy treatment manual for clients*. New York: Guilford Press.

Leahy, H. and Holland, S. (2000) *Treatment Plans and Interventions for Depression and Anxiety Disorders*. New York: Guilford Press.

McMullin, R.E. (1996) *Handbook of Cognitive Therapy Techniques*. New York: Norton.

Padesky, C.A. (1994) 'Schema change processes in cognitive therapy'. *Clinical Psychology and Psychotherapy*, 1(5): 267–78.

Palmer, S. and Szymanska, K. (2007) 'Cognitive Behavioural Coaching; An Integrative Approach'. In S. Palmer and A. Whybrow (eds) *Handbook of Coaching Psychology: A Guide for Practitioners*. London: Sage.

Szymanska, K. (2008) 'The Downward Arrow Technique'. *The Coaching Psychologist*, 4(2): 85–6.

Szymanska, K. (2009) 'The case for assessment and case conceptualization in coaching'. *Coaching Psychology International*, 2(1): 6–9.

Szymanska, K. and Palmer, S. (2009) *Introduction to Counselling and Psychotherapy: The Essential Guide*. London: Routledge.

Chapter 3

Bennett-Levy, J., Butler, G., Fennell, M., Hackmann, A., Mueller, M. and Westbrook, D. (2004) *Oxford Guide to Behavioural Experiments*. Oxford: Oxford University Press.

Palmer, S. and Neenan, M. (1998) 'Double imagery procedure'. *Rational Emotive Behaviour Therapist*, 6(2): 89–92.

Szymanska, K. (2009) 'Behavioural Assignments'. *The Coaching Psychologist*, 5(2): 130–1.

Chapter 4

Cooper, C. and Palmer, P. (2000) *Conquer Your Stress*. London: CIPD.

Lazarus, A.A. (1982) *Personal enrichment through imagery*. (Cassette recording.) New York: BMA Audio-cassettes/Guilford.

Lazarus, A.A. (1984) *In the Mind's Eye*. New York: Guilford Press.

McMullin, R. (2000) *Handbook of Cognitive Therapy Techniques*. New York: Norton.

Palmer, S. (1993) *Multimodal Techniques: Relaxation and Hypnosis*. London: Centre for Stress Management and Centre for Multimodal Therapy.

Palmer, S. (2008) 'Coping imagery'. *The Coaching Psychologist*, 4(2): 39.

Palmer, S. (2009) 'Compassion focused imagery for use within compassion focused coaching'. *Coaching Psychology International*, 2(9): 13.

Palmer, S. and Neenan, M. (1998) 'Double Imagery Procedure'. *The Rational Emotive Behaviour Therapist*, 6(2): 89–92.

Palmer, S. and Strickland, L. (1996) *Stress Management: A Quick Guide*. Dunstable: Folens.

Palmer, S., Cooper, C. and Thomas, K. (2003) *Creating a Balance: Managing Stress*. London: The British Library.

Szymanska, K. (2008) 'Time Projection Imagery'. *The Coaching Psychologist*, 4(3): 186–7.

Chapter 5

O'Broin, A. and Palmer, S. (2008) *Panic Disorder: What, who, why and how to help?* Leicester: British Psychological Society. Free download: http://www.bps.org.uk/sites/default/files/documents/panic_disorder_information_leaflet.pdf

Palmer, S. and O'Broin, A. (2008) *Phobias: What, who, why and how to help?* Leicester: British Psychological Society. Free download: http://www.bps.org.uk/sites/default/files/documents/phobias_information_leaflet.pdf

Szymanska, K. and Palmer, S. (2000) 'Cognitive counselling and psychotherapy' in S. Palmer (ed.) *Introduction to Counselling and Psychotherapy: The Essential Guide*. London: Sage.

Chapter 6

Chang, E. (2000) 'Perfectionism as a predictor of positive and negative psychological outcomes. Examining a mediation model in younger and older adults'. *Journal of Counseling Psychology*, 47(1): 0022–0167.

Davey, G.C.L. (1994) 'Pathological worrying as exacerbated problem-solving'. In G. Davey and F. Tallis (eds) *Worrying Perspectives on Theory, Assessment and Treatment*. Chichester: Wiley.

Flower Associates International (2011) Personal communication, 12 August.

Leahy, R.L. and Holland, S.J. (2000) *Treatment Plans and Interventions for Depression and Anxiety Disorders*. New York: Guilford Press.

McLaughlin, K., Borkovec, Y. and Sibrava, N. (2007) 'The effects of worry and rumination on affect styles and cognitive acclivity'. *Behaviour Therapy*, 38(1): 23–38.

MacLeod, A.K. (1994) 'Worry and explanation-based pessimism'. In G. Davey and F. Tallis (eds) *Worrying Perspectives on Theory, Assessment and Treatment*. Chichester: Wiley.

O'Hanian, V. (2007) Personal communication, 12 January.

Tallis, F., Davey, G.C.L., and Capuzzo, N. (1994) 'The phenomenology of non-pathological worry: a preliminary investigation'. In G. Davey and F. Tallis (eds) *Worrying Perspectives on Theory, Assessment and Treatment*. Chichester: Wiley.

Chapter 7

Grbcic, S. and Palmer, S. (2007) 'A cognitive-behavioural self-help approach to stress management and prevention at work: a randomised controlled trial'. *The Rational Emotive Behaviour Therapist*, 12(1): 41–3.

Gyllensten, K. and Palmer, S. (2005) 'Working with a Client Suffering From Workplace Stress in a Primary Care Setting: A Cognitive Behavioural Case Study'. *Counselling Psychology Review*, 20: 4–14.

Health and Safety Executive (2011) Statistics – working days lost. Retrieved 20 January 2012 from www.hse.gov.uk/statistics/dayslost.htm.

Health and Safety Executive (2011) Work-related stress – stress and mental health at work. Retrieved 20 January 2012 from www.hse.gov.uk/stress/furtheradvice/stressandmentalhealth.htm

Neenan, M. and Dryden, W. (2002) *Coaching: A Cognitive Behavioural Approach*. London: Routledge.

Oliver, P. J. and Lewis, L. (2003) 'Strike out Stress'. *Occupational Health*, 61(9): 24–5.

Osipow, S.H. and Spokane, A.R. (1987) *Manual for the Occupational Stress Inventory*. Odessa, FL: Psychological Assessment Resources.

Palmer, S. and Strickland, L. (1996) *Stress Management: A Quick Guide*. Dunstable: Folens.

Palmer, S., Cooper, C. and Thomas, K. (2001) 'Model of organisational stress for use within an occupational health education/promotion or wellbeing programme – A short communication'. *Health Education Journal*, 60(4): 378–80.

Palmer, S., Cooper, C., and Thomas, K. (2003) *Creating a Balance: Managing stress*. London: The British Library.

Rosenman, R.H., Brand, R.J., Jenkins, C.D., Friedman, M., Straus, R. and Wurm, M. (1975) 'Coronary heart disease in the Western Collaborative Group Study. Final follow-up experience of 8.5 years'. *Journal of American Medical Association*, 22: 872–7.

Rotter, J.B. (1966) 'Generalised expectancies for internal versus external control of reinforcement'. *Psychology Monographs. General and Applied*, 80: 1–26.

Szymanska, K. (2008) 'The Downward Arrow Technique'. *The Coaching Psychologist*, 4(2): 85–6.

Wilding, C. and Palmer, S. (2010) *Beat Self-esteem with CBT*. London: Teach Yourself.

Chapter 8

Deffenbacher, J. (1996) 'Cognitive-Behavioral Approaches to Anger Management'. In K. Dobson and K. Craig (eds) *Advances in Cognitive Behavioral Therapy*. California: Sage.

McMullin, M. (2000) *The New Handbook of Cognitive Therapy Techniques*. New York: Norton.

Chapter 9

Richards, D. and Lovell, K. (1999) 'Behavioural and cognitive behavioural interventions in the treatment of PTSD'. In W. Yule (ed.) *Post Traumatic Stress Disorders: Concepts and therapy*. Chichester: Wiley.

Chapter 10

Elizabeth Finn Care (2010) New report highlights devastating effect recession has had on UK's mental health. Retrieved 21 January 2012, from www.elizabethfinncare.org.uk/Rise_in_mental_health_illness

MIND (2010) 'Prevelance of mental health problems in Great Britain'. Retrieved 15 August, 2010 from www.mind.org.uk/help/research_and_policy/statistics_1_how_common_is_mental_distress#prevalence

Wei, M., Heppner, P., and Brent, H. (2003) 'Perceived coping as a mediator between attachment and psychological distress: A structured equation modeling approach'. *Journal of Counseling Psychology*, 4(50): 438–47.

World Health Organization (WHO) (2010). 'What is depression?' Retrieved 15 August, 2010, from www.who.int/mental_health/management/depression/definition/en/

Chapter 11

Escartına, J., Rodriguez-Carballeira, A., Zapf, D., Porrua, C. and Martın-Pena, J. (2009) 'Perceived severity of various bullying behaviours at work and the relevance of exposure to bullying'. *Work and Stress*, 23(3): 191–205.

Quine, L. (1999) 'Workplace bullying in NHS Community Trust: staff questionnaire survey'. *British Medical Journal*, 318(7178): 318–28.

Randall, P. (1997) *Adult Bullying: Perpetrators and victims*. London: Routledge.

Tehrani, N. (2004) 'Bullying: a source of chronic post-traumatic stress'. *British Journal of Guidance and Counselling*, 12(3).

WBI (2010) Results of the 2010 WBI US Workplace Bullying Survey. Retrieved 1 September 2011 from www.workplacebullying.org/wbiresearch/2010-wbi-national-survey/

Chapter 12

Centre for Stress Management (2005) Primary Certificate in Assertion and Communication Skills Training. London: Centre for Coaching in association with Centre for Stress Management.

Smith, M.J. (1975) *When I Say No I Feel Guilty*. New York: Dial.

Chapter 13

Cooper, C. and Palmer, S. (2000) *Conquer your stress*. London: CIPD.

Neenan, M. (2012) 'Understanding and tacking procrastination'. In M. Neenan and S. Palmer (eds), *Cognitive Behavioural Coaching in Practice: An evidence based approach*. Hove: Routledge.

Palmer, S. and Cooper, C. (2010) *How to Deal with Stress* (2nd edn). London: Kogan Page.

Sapadin, L. and Maguire, J. (1996) *It's About Time: The six steps of procrastination and how to overcome them*. New York: Penguin.

Chapter 14

Palmer, S. and Cooper, C. (2010) *How to Deal with Stress* (2nd edn). London: Kogan Page.

Palmer, S. and Puri, A. (2006) *Coping with Stress at University: A Survival Guide*. London: Sage.

INDEX

NB numbers in *italics* indicate figures or tables